Grafting Memory

Essays on War and Commemoration

Commonwealth War Graves Collection, undated photo.

Grafting Memory

Essays on War and Commemoration

Bill Lipke ▪ Bill Mares

Bill Lipke (signature)

Bill Mares (signature)

BARD OWL BOOKS

Shelburne, Vermont 05482

Cover and book design by Laurie Thomas

ISBN: 978-1-935922-84-1
Library of Congress Control Number: 2015949102

Published by Bard Owl Books
An imprint of Voices of Vermonters Publishing Group, Inc.
PO Box 595
Shelburne, Vermont 05482

"I was the first fruits of the battle of Missionary Ridge.
When I felt the bullet enter my heart
I wished I had staid at home and gone to jail
For stealing the hogs of Curl Trenary,
Instead of running away and joining the army.
Rather a thousand times the county jail
Than to lie under this marble figure with wings,
And this granite pedestal Bearing the words, *'Pro Patria.'*
What do they mean, anyway?"

[Edgar Lee Masters, "Knowlt Hoheimer"
from *Spoon River Anthology,* 1915]

"The objection can be raised that … the dead are still 'being used for the living,' They
are to help us, to change us. That is perhaps true … but is any other relationship with
the dead conceivable? Doesn't all remembering of them and praying for them …
have this character, that we 'need' the dead in a double sense of wanting them and of
making use of them? They have been taken from us and are unable to prevent this use
of themselves. But there is no way to love them other than to incorporate them into
our work at living."

[Dorothee Soelle, from *Suffering,* 1975]

Contents

Grafting Memory

Foreword

IN *GRAFTING MEMORY,* my close friends and colleagues Bill Lipke and Bill Mares have written a fascinating study about war memorials both familiar and virtually unknown, objects that we walk or drive past without a thought. Perceptive, analytical, emotional, inspiring, it prompts us to ask questions about both war and its monuments. It asks us to stop, to use our eyes searchingly (Lipke is an art historian, Mares a photographer and history teacher), and ask ourselves about the battles these monuments enshrine. Who chose the subjects, contracted the artists and builders, picked the commemorative, noble words that are engraved on them? Who decided how to pay for them? What civic/provincial/national officials squabbled over their particular features? Perhaps most important: what do they mean *now* to those who fought in these actions? To those who survived? How do they honor the dead? This is the ultimate challenge that Lipke and Mares lay before us. With this book as a field guide of sorts, many readers will look with new eyes upon things which tell all too much about both war and the historical memories embedded therein.

Grafting Memory, to its credit, challenges its readers to find their own questions, which will prompt more queries than answers. It reminded me that Canada's war memorials and monuments were of little interest to me as a child. Occasionally I was taken to watch the Toronto Scottish Regiment's church parade—ah, those pipers! But I took very little note of the grey, unspeaking statues sprinkled around Toronto.

Television brought coverage of national ceremonies for Armistice Day, but I failed to understand what that they had to say to me. Only one of my uncles had served abroad, becoming both deaf and an alcoholic in the process—the rest, including my Dad, worked in "war industries." Miraculously, I knew no friends with family members who had died in action, and despite the efforts of my school teachers to inform us as to the deeper, underlying meanings of war in general, and WWI and WWII in particular, I knew or cared little about international conflict. We learned of Canada's coming of age on Vimy Ridge (commemorated by Walter Allward's magnificent memorial), but little was said of the artistic or storytelling elements involved in memorial-building.

In 1954, I became a university student in a Canada eager to put the horror of war behind it. We sought a brave, new world to follow the second "War to end all Wars." North Americans in the '50s were not well acquainted with Post Traumatic Stress Disorder (although many WWII warriors suffered from it). I went off to the States to finish my formal education, then took a job teaching—of all things—Canadian Studies. I saw that Americans commemorated all their wars as triumphs of the "victors valiant." They paid homage to great US victories, choosing to remain in denial of the clear fact that the Korean "conflict" had been, after all, a major war, and almost lost. The Iwo Jima flag-raising photo became a patriotic icon which took solid form as a Marine memorial at Arlington Cemetery. The Vietnam Memorial, possibly the greatest, most poignant war memorial ever designed, was conceived in controversy but proved tremendously moving once seen. America waited a long time, however, to memorialize WWII and that conflict in Korea. Sadly, we now wonder what future monuments will remind us of the horrors of the War on Terror and other far-flung conflagrations. How will tomorrow's artists respond to such challenges? Shall we want them to try? There are other kinds of war memorials, of course. Listen, for example, to Benjamin Britten's *War Requiem* celebrating the rebuilding of Coventry Cathedral, using Wilfred Owen's scarifying poetry to deflate "that old lie, *dulce et decorum pro patria mori.*"

Our world is again in a parlous state, war the dominant, most discussed "solution" to problems which might be cured were all politicians to work to find real solutions without shouldering once more the guns. Perhaps we should all look more keenly at that grey old statue of a warrior (named or "Unknown") in your town square and think about what it *really* means in the early twenty-first century. Perhaps it is time to reread Wilfred Owen's poetry, or listen to what Britten (a conscientious objector) composed to remind us that, while the enduring triumph of war is often death itself, men and women throughout history have sung compelling songs of heroism and sacrifice and, ultimately, of truth and strange beauty.

But first read *Grafting Memory*, which will challenge you to look closely, to hear wonders, to remember what this is all about … and never to forget that "In Flanders fields the poppies blow, between the crosses, row on row…"

—William Metcalfe

William Metcalfe is Professor Emeritus of History, University of Vermont, where he served as chair of the departments of History and Music, and was for ten years the director of Canadian Studies. For sixteen years, he served as the editor of the American Review of Canadian Studies. *He was awarded the Donner Foundation Medal for distinguished contributions to Canadian Studies in the US. Co-founder of the UVM Baroque Ensemble, the Burlington G&S Singers, the Vermont Mozart Festival, and the Oriana Singers of Vermont, he continues in retirement as a conductor.*

Preface *Bill Lipke*

MY PARENTS SHARED a tall, dark mahogany dresser in their bedroom. Two small drawers at the top contained personal items belonging to each. Mom's was the top right drawer. I remember her opening the drawer when I was five or six to show me two beribboned medals that she said belonged to her father, whom I had never met. They were medals from the First World War roughly the size of an American silver dollar with low relief images over which I rubbed my fingers. Now I know them to have been the British War Medal (King George VI on his horse, trampling Death) and a Great War for Civilization Victory Medal (winged Victory with her left arm extended, her right carrying a sheaf of olive branches). Many years later, I asked to see them again. "They're gone," Mom said. No explanation. The medals had simply disappeared. Somehow I knew they had been thrown away. But why? There would be more unanswered questions. Why had my grandfather joined the Canadian Expeditionary Force in 1917 and gone off to war, abandoning his wife and young daughter? Had he been injured? Where did he live now?

Some of those questions were answered in 1947 when I met my grandfather Ross Wilson Prentiss for the first and only time in Gravenhurst, Ontario, where he lived his last years at the Muskoka Tuberculosis Sanitarium—a facility also used by Canadian war veterans gassed during the Great War. I was eleven years old at the time, and that trip to Canada created a lasting impression as we stopped to "view" the Dionne Quintuplets (sadly, a tourist attraction of that era). The experiences of a once-seen grandfather *and* a "biological rarity"—both literally fenced off and fenced in from the rest of the world—were departures from my usual adolescent experiences. A year later, in 1948, Grandpa Prentiss died at the Sanitorium. He was fifty-nine; a belated casualty of the Great War.

I learned much later that another family member, William Franklin Lipke, my Dad's oldest brother, had also served in the First War, enlisting in the US Navy early in 1918. Asked about his whereabouts (I was curious because we shared the same name), I was told in a tightlipped response that he had "disappeared." I never met Uncle Bill. Like my grandfather, Uncle Bill's marriage also ended in divorce. He, too, had abandoned his wife and family, moving from Wisconsin in the 1930s to the Pacific Northwest where he died in 1961, an incurable alcoholic.

One might conclude that both Prentiss and Lipke went off to the Great War in Europe to avoid the problems and routines of everyday life at home. Theirs were voluntary enlistments; neither was conscripted. For them, the Great War "over-there" was the kind of escape so aptly described by F. Scott Fitzgerald in 1926 in "Winter Dreams." In it, Fitzgerald described one character as "one of those young thousands who greeted the war with a certain amount of relief, welcoming the liberation from webs of tangled emotion."

What seems clear to me now is that both family veterans were unable to return to civilian life "present and accounted for." They remained missing in action, their lives altered by their war experiences. They were amongst the hundreds of thousands of veterans who physically survived wars but were incapable of being fully present to their lives when they returned. No monuments or memorials have or will be erected to acknowledge the chaos and havoc war has created for them and for their families. The reader might thereby correctly conclude that my interest in the topics of war and commemoration is personal.

The study of monuments and memorials would also become professional. In the early 1960s, I began graduate studies in art history, developing an enthusiasm for the philosophical issues of cultural commemoration. My specific interest in First World War art and architectural monuments grew out of questions raised forty-five years earlier while completing research for a doctoral dissertation on early twentieth-century British artists inspired by cubism and futurism who called themselves Vorticists. Many of them and artists of that era were awarded commissions to paint assigned subjects associated with the Great War for the Canadian and British War Memorials schemes. Both projects were initiated by Canadian newspaper magnate Max Aitken (Lord Beaverbrook) and directed by London art critic Paul G. Konody.

Surely, I speculated, the artists hired by Konody might have to make aesthetic compromises when undertaking public commissions, especially the more radical members of the Vorticist coterie. Both projects, to their credit, engaged artists whose styles collectively represented a broad range of responses to the subjects of war, from academic figurative painting to cubist-futurist inspired canvases. Thus, a careful study of the British and Canadian projects would present both a uniquely broad survey of British and Canadian art of the early twentieth-century and a comprehensive record of all aspects of the Great War, from battlefield to home front. Today one can view the results of the artists' efforts at the Imperial War Museum and the Tate Britain (Millbank) in London; and the Canadian War Museum and National Gallery of Canada in Ottawa.

When I accepted an academic appointment at the University of Vermont in 1970 I was fortunate to be invited to participate in the interdisciplinary Canadian Studies program. Here was an opportunity to teach Canadian art and architecture and a stimulus to continue my research of the eight hundred or so works for the Canadian War Memorials Project housed in Ottawa, only four hours away. Sabbatical leaves funded by the University and the Canadian Government made it possible to study firsthand both the materials in Ottawa and the related monuments, memorials, and cemeteries of the Great War in England, France, and Belgium.

Early on and along the way I met Bill Mares, who was working as a journalist and later as teacher in the Greater Burlington area. We shared many mutual interests, quickly became friends, and over some thirty plus years have explored together what has become a fruitful research into the vast subject of monuments, memorials, and commemoration. I am especially indebted to his longstanding query to me ("So when am I going to see what you have written about the First War?") which prompted me to put pen to paper once again. These collaborative essays are a result of a long standing friendship and many, many hours of pleasant discourse and discussion over tea and some first-rate local pastries.

Grafting Memory

Preface *Bill Mares*

THE IDEA WAS Bill's. The book is ours.

I met Bill in the late 1970s when, as a reporter, I was sent up to the University of Vermont's art museum to write a story about its collection. Bill was then both a professor of art history and the museum director. We have been neighbors, fellow singers, and intellectual soulmates ever since. Our shared interest in war memorials and monuments developed when we both read Paul Fussell's *The Great War and Modern Memory*—a powerful description of how a generation of poets struggled to find the language to encompass the wretchedness of the trenches and the epic slaughter of World War I.

Like Bill, I've lived life on war's sidelines. I've had the fascination for combat that often afflicts the non-combatant. From the moment I was old enough to comprehend it, my mother would tell me I was born on the night that the Nazis bombed Coventry Cathedral in November 1940. My first memories were of wartime in peaceful St. Louis, with its paper and can drives, the black-out curtains, the savings bond stamps, the ration cards. For our gang games, the neighborhood became by turns the fields of France, the mountains of Italy, and the beaches of the Pacific. Our imaginary guns fell silent only with the news of the real deaths of neighbor boys at Anzio, Normandy, and Tarawa. I was playing under our piano when Roosevelt's death was announced over the radio, and I was just going to bed when my brother rushed into our room to speak of an "atomic bomb!"

As we boys grew up, my brother took after our father's interest in science. I followed my mother into the study of history and current affairs. My mother drilled me to learn the layers of sacrifice, tragedy, and triumph that comprised history. Our house was a library with books of every kind. Among the thousands of volumes that filled our shelves was a thick volume about three times the size of a Bible. Its spine was broken and pages were constantly slipping out. It was an encyclopedia of World War I, and on the title page was the real signature of Captain William "Billy" Bishop—a Canadian pilot and winner of the Victoria Cross and numerous other medals. When I touched that autograph, it was an inky link to history, and I could imagine the hand that wrote that name had pulled the trigger of his Vickers machine gun.

Years later, after college, I joined the Marine Corps Reserves, and after three failed career choices, I fell into journalism—both written and photographic. None of my Marine Corps Reserve units was ever called to active duty in that tumultuous period of the Vietnam War. But my fascination with the military remained, and when I completed my six-year obligation in 1968, I asked the Marine Corps if I could spend three months at USMC Recruit Depot Parris Island, South

Carolina, doing a photographic essay about the training of one platoon. The Marine Corps agreed. After two years of work, my first book, *The Marine Machine*, was published.

Then, in 1998, I got a chance to see some of the fields of slaughter with my own eyes. With my father-in-law (a combat historian of World War II) and my twelve-year-old son, I traveled the battlefields of France and Belgium—from Normandy to Waterloo. The most moving were the monuments and cemeteries of the First World War—the Somme, Verdun, Château Thierry. To see field upon tranquil field, row upon row of markers and headstones lined up as the troops had been lined up to go over the top to death or disfigurement was a breathtaking experience. At Beaumont Hamel, where in thirty minutes an entire battalion of Newfoundlanders was mowed down like wheat, the trenches remained, with a few of the original barbed wire hangers still stuck up like skeletal arms of the dead.

We visited Thiepval, the massive monument to the unknown dead, on the Somme River. There are 73,000 names carved on its many planes, giving the double anonymity of uniformity and unmarked death. At Verdun, atop a hill sits the vast Ossuary: part church spire, part submarine, part Quonset hut. It was skirted around with 12,000 graves. Among the crosses are hundreds of Muslim crescents to mark the graves of Moroccan and Algerian dead. Below the Ossuary itself, you walk through an eerily lit vault and look down through Plexiglas at some of the bones of over 120,000 French and German soldiers never identified.

As we drove across France, every town had its monument to *poilus* from that vicinity. It reminded me of driving through New England, where village upon village proudly displayed its monument to the soldiers of our Civil War.

After reading Fussell's *The Great War and Modern Memory* with Bill, I became so hooked on the subject of memorializing with words that over the next year I read the memoirs of Edmund Blunden, Robert Graves, Siegfried Sassoon, David Jones, and several others. Like a good teacher, Bill then moved me on from poetry to the role of physical monuments in the collective and individual memory. In our exchanges, Bill would periodically refer to his work about the Canadian War Memorial. I had never heard of it. Was it a building? Well, no. A collection? Not exactly. It was an assembly of Canadian artists' responses to World War I. Bill's interest had grown out of his PhD. work on a group of artists known as the Vorticists. Some of their works were included in the memorial. Once Bill began visiting the Ottawa and Montréal of their account, he learned of the larger Canadian effort to memorialize their Great War experience. He told me how Canada had become a distinct nation through its Great War test of fire.

Over the years, I occasionally asked Bill to read some of my book chapters, essays, or radio commentaries on different topics. His comments were so warm that I began asking him to show me some of *his* writings about the Canadian project. Months, years passed. Nothing. He always had some excuse. Finally, one Wednesday afternoon at the beginning of our choral practice, he dropped a thick manila envelope on my lap and said simply, "See what you think."

That night, like a bank robber who has cleaned out a safe, I sat down to look through the loot of lecture notes, book reviews, and essays about memorials and cemeteries of World War I. The essays had evocative titles: "Suffering, Loss and Bereavement," "Do Monuments Matter?" "Memorials to the Missing and the Unknown Dead," "Burial with Honor: Cemeteries of the Imperial War Graves Commission." Like any good academic, he had plentiful questions and a few tentative, thoughtful answers. Back and forth, he plowed the fields of the war dead and their memorials, turning up new ideas like the bones I saw at Verdun or the names at Thiepval.

There was the seed of a book here, one that could explore again the efforts to commemorate the horrific war whose hundredth anniversary was approaching. Maybe Bill could compare these memorials with those of the Civil War. (After all we were in the middle of *its* sesquicentennial.) And maybe I could help. I made an inventory of my potential contributions, of what I knew and what I wanted to know. My work in photojournalism and fascination with war photography could play a role, I imagined. Most importantly, I knew how to write books. I had already co-authored books with four other people. I had just finished writing one, in fact, and I was feeling that familiar itch to play in the space between the subjective and the objective. E.M. Forster's directive, "Only connect," had long been my maxim; I love making connections, and connecting with history is in my blood stream.

Bill began sending me off on field trips to learn that monuments were more than stone and bronze, more than pigeons' latrines. He took me to the Shaw on Boston Common, to the War Memorial in Ottawa, to local statues of Ethan Allen and Civil War Generals Wells and Stannard. He got me thinking about *why* people put up these monuments. When did abstraction supplant representation? Why was the Vietnam Veterans Memorial's commemoration of a defeat more successful than the World War II Memorial's was in victory?

Several months after he gave me that fateful envelope, Bill and I met for a pre-choral practice coffee. I told him that he had the beginnings of a compelling work of cultural history. "It would be a crime against your profession and all you've invested in the Canadian project not to make something of it," I said. "I'd like to help. I can bring my journalist and historian's eyes to your aesthetic sensibilities. You can take the lead, of course. But in time, I might learn enough to make a few original contributions. It'll be a great ride." He thought about my proposition for a week and then said yes.

And that's how this collaboration began.

Ypres Military Cemetery, Belgium

Introduction

"And some there be, which have no memorial; who are perished, as though they had never been; and are become as though they had never been born; and their children after them."—Ecclesiasticus 44:9

"The whole Earth is the Sepulchre of famous men; and their story is not graven only on Stone over their native earth, but lives on far away, without visible symbol, woven into the stuff of other men's lives."—Thucydides

IN THE NOVEMBER 13,1995 issue of *The New Yorker* magazine, there appeared a remarkable short story about the aftermath of World War I and the effects on one survivor. In "Evermore," Julian Barnes asks the reader to consider the possibility that with time's passing, we might forget the sacrifices and memorials to the Great War. The title of Barnes' story is derived from a biblical passage that Rudyard Kipling persuaded the British Imperial War Graves Commission (IWGC) to inscribe on the Stone of Remembrance in all IWGC cemeteries: "Their name liveth for evermore." Barnes' principal character, the sister of a young British soldier killed in that war, ponders if in the future there might be an end to remembering—"Nevermore" rather than "Evermore."

The story unfolds with the sister's yearly pilgrimage to visit the grave of her brother, Private Samuel M. Moss, who was killed on January 21, 1917 and buried in the Cabaret Rouge military cemetery in France. He is one of three British soldiers identified as Jewish by the Star of David amongst the seven thousand gravestones in the cemetery. She becomes a "connoisseur of grief," obsessed with keeping her brother's memory alive. She brings English turf and flowers to plant in front of the headstone. She requests permission to sleep in the cemetery next to her brother's grave; to have her remains scattered next to the headstone of her brother when she dies. The authorities say no to all of her requests.

Time passes. The brother's gravestone literally becomes a touchstone on his sister's annual trek. For her, his name indeed "liveth for evermore." Monuments and cemeteries to the newly fallen soldiers of World War II affront the sister. The Jewish gravestones in Cabaret Rouge are desecrated. Nevertheless, she remains faithful to her brother's memory, returning to his grave in an annual ritual.

"Evermore" became a *literary* touchstone for us and gave us this book's title—a "grafting" of memory from one generation to the next. From the study of this "architecture and sculpture of grief" emerged our first theme. To seal their memories, survivors and succeeding generations engaged in three principle actions: encounters, rituals, and pilgrimages. Each of these will appear and reappear in this book.

On the Gettysburg battlefield, Abraham Lincoln spoke to the futility of building memorials to the dead ("We cannot dedicate, we cannot consecrate, we cannot hallow this ground. The brave men, living and dead, who struggled here, have consecrated it far above our poor power to add or detract…"). But the survivors erected monuments and memorials anyway, and in a host of ways.

Governments have always had an overweening pride and shared it with chosen generals and leaders through commemorative obelisks, triumphal arches, and equestrian statues. Only in the nineteenth century, after the American Civil War, did governments begin to take on a kind of collective survivors' guilt that moved them to honor and bury their war dead in national and local cemeteries. This is the second theme of this book—how the American Civil War and the Great War of 1914-1918 together launched new practices for honoring the dead as individuals. Some of these practices included the uniformity of burial of officers and men, the naming of the dead, memorials to the missing, individual recognition in photos and statuary, photographic records, and living memorials. These new practices fed off each other, creating an atmosphere that honored the enlisted soldier as never before.

In the Civil War and World War I, the memorials were democratized to the point that names of the dead were listed not just in cemeteries or on battlefields but on village greens in places like St. Albans, Vermont and Concord, Massachusetts; the Victorian and Albert Museum and Paddington Railway Station in London; and in towns and cities throughout Canada. The generic (iconic) forms of each war's memorials became idiosyncratic and individual.

The third theme of this book examines how memory has been grafted on succeeding generations through memorials and visible symbols (utilitarian or otherwise) so that the honoring of war dead will not be forgotten or obscured by the accretions of history. To complicate this matter, as wars become more contentious, there seems to be less agreement on what monuments about them should say—or even if they are needed.

Along the way we try to answer a number of questions. For example: How have countless streams of private grief joined the main stem of public mourning? How have monuments been used for nation building? How has the memorial landscape changed from the nearly ubiquitous standing Civil War monument, to the World War I doughboys, to almost nothing? How can a memorial to an unpopular war (Vietnam) be so popular? Like archaeologists, we propose to get out the trowel, brush, and sieve to examine and reassemble the fragments of memory that become "stones of nationhood and identity."

Writing this book has taken us to the churchyards of Britain, the battlefields of France, the American cemeteries of North and South, the village greens and city squares of many towns in Canada and the United States. We offer a collection of essays primarily about sculptural and architectural memorials and monuments, but paintings and photographs also figure prominently in our discussion.

Simply living in Vermont has given us a vivid perspective on memorials. Our state's memorial history begins with the Revolution and continues to the present War on Terror. Many of the monuments and memorials far beyond our state's borders were built with Vermont marble and granite. And it is with the monument landscape of the University of Vermont that we now begin.

—Bill Lipke and Bill Mares

Grafting Memory

CHAPTER ONE

Monument Makers of the American Revolution

IN THE 1870s, the Revolutionary War of 1773-1783 was brought to the forefront of the nation's memory with extensive celebrations of its one-hundredth anniversary. The Centennial Fair of 1876 held in Philadelphia, officially opened by President Ulysses S. Grant, sparked renewed interest in that historic period. The Fair reminded a younger generation of Americans that in spite of the superior military and naval forces of Great Britain, bands of revolutionary citizens— the minutemen, the Green Mountain Boys, and other citizen soldiers—had successfully defeated the British militia and gained their independence. Together with European sympathizers and proponents of democracy who had come to the aid of the colonists, these revolutionaries transformed themselves from colonies beholden to Great Britain into an independent political entity called the United States of America. Not the least of those citizen soldiers was a Virginian named George Washington, general of the Continental Army, whose commemorative monument on the Mall was begun in 1848 but was stopped in 1854 due to shortage of funds. In the patriotic spirit of the Centennial, Congress voted on July 5, 1876 to fund and complete the monument that was finally dedicated on February 21, 1885.

We begin this series of essays with a study of two works: one well-known, the other hidden from plain sight on a northern New England campus. Their execution and completion was also stimulated by the Centennial fever that swept the country in the 1870s and 1880s—a movement fueled by the realization that the Union had come close to dissolution with the deadly Civil War of the previous decade.

The marking of time with anniversary celebrations is one of several ways of "grafting memory." Marking the place where important events took place is another. Both actions depend upon individuals who find the ways and means to incite their fellow citizens to create memorials to mark the key events and persons of the past.

THE PATRONS

Ebenezer Hubbard from Concord, Massachusetts, and John Purple Howard of Burlington, Vermont, shared similar concerns regarding the war of the American Revolution, a conflict which to them had not been adequately commemorated. Both men felt the memory of the Revolutionary War was becoming a distant, even displaced, event. They feared it

THE MINUTE MAN. CONCORD. MASS.

Daniel Chester French, *The Minute Man*, 1873-75. Concord, Massachusetts. Postcard, 1947. (Courtesy Lantern Press)

was being eclipsed by the recent Civil War—with its staggering death toll and projected manifold forms of commemoration (battlefield memorials, public monuments, and national cemeteries). Seeking to correct this "historical amnesia," Hubbard and Howard commissioned major statues commemorating the Revolutionary War—statues whose siting and placement were as significant as the symbolic content of the work itself. Because of their generosity as private patrons, two significant monuments to heroes of the Revolution came into being.

THE MINUTE MAN (1871-1875)

The Minute Man by sculptor Daniel Chester French of Concord, Massachusetts, is today the best-known monument to the citizen soldier of the American Revolution. The statue was originally commissioned by the town of Concord to mark the Centennial of the Battle of Concord (April 19,1775). The battle had previously been commemorated in the 1830s, both with a stone monument erected in the rough form of an obelisk placed at the site of the skirmish, and by Ralph Waldo Emerson's poem entitled "Concord Hymn," composed for the occasion of the erection of that marker. Funds for the 1873 commission of a monument to designate the one-hundredth anniversary of the Battle of Concord had been designated in the will of longtime Concord resident Ebenezer Hubbard. Hubbard argued that the exact place where the minutemen militia fought had not been marked and should be for the Centennial. This was on the opposite side from the North Bridge held by the British forces and designated earlier by the obelisk of 1836. A committee of ten—including Ralph Waldo Emerson, a resident of Concord now well into his seventies—selected the young, relatively unknown sculptor Daniel Chester French to execute the commission. The committee stipulated that the first stanza of Emerson's 1836 poem should be inscribed on the base of the completed work:

> By the rude bridge that arched the flood,
> Their flag to April's breeze unfurled,
> Here once the embattled farmers stood,
> And fired the shot heard round the world.

Initially offering to complete the statue at his own cost, French was reimbursed with the monies provided by Hubbard's gift when the committee saw the completed work. It was dedicated on April 19, 1875.

The Minute Man was an immediate success, so much so that, in keeping with the enthusiasm marking the one-hundredth anniversary of the founding of the Republic, a cast of French's Concord statue was displayed at the Centennial Fair in Philadelphia in 1876. The image of the statue has since appeared on postage stamps, war bonds, and various commercial advertisements; it is an image as familiar to Americans as that of Uncle Sam.

French's iconic statue is a starkly realistic rendering of a Massachusetts farmer/soldier: plow at his feet, gun in hand, shirt sleeves rolled, and striking a resolute stance modeled after the pose of the antique classical statue *Apollo Belvedere*. The work owed an aesthetic debt as well to the distinguished American sculptor, John Quincy Adams Ward, a mentor with whom French had briefly studied. French consulted with Ward at the commencement of his commission, and Ward's advice to his young protégé was to make the work so grand

Concord Battle Monument, 1837. With view of North Bridge, Concord, Massachusetts. Photograph.

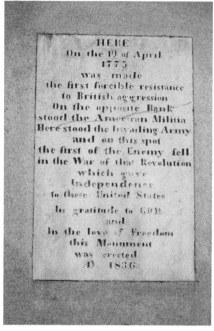

Detail—inscription on pedestal, *Concord Battle Monument*, 1837. Photograph.

The Minute Man, 1925. Commemorative postage stamp with Emerson's 1837 poem celebrating the fiftieth anniversary of the erection of the statue. (US Postal Service)

3

that ladies would bring their jewelry to melt them down to cast the Minute Man. The ladies did not have to bring their goods to be melted down, however, as a legislative bill was passed authorizing cannon from the Civil War just nine years past to be used for the casting. At the material level, *The Minute Man* was literally a functional monument to the Civil War. Of greater import, it was a symbolic monument to the Massachusetts citizen militia who fought at the North Bridge one hundred years earlier. Erected on the actual site where the American militia fought the British, *The Minute Man* stands on the side of the North Bridge, facing the early obelisk marking the place held by the British, functioning precisely as Ebenezer Hubbard had directed in his will.

The success of *The Minute Man* led to a series of important public and private commissions for French, among which were monuments and memorials commemorating individuals and events of the Civil War and the Great War (1914-1918). These included the striking Melvin Memorial ("Mourning Victory," Sleepy Hollow Cemetery, Concord, 1906-1908) commissioned by James Melvin in memory of his three brothers killed in the Civil War in which he had also served, and the monument to Commodore George H. Perkins, commander of the Union gunboat *Cayuga*. This latter commission was a collaboration with architect Henry Bacon for the New Hampshire State House in Concord in 1902—a working relationship which culminated in their most famous and memorable work, *The Lincoln Memorial* for the Mall, Washington, D.C., dedicated in 1922.

French's commissions for memorials and monuments to the Great War included the St. Paul's School war memorial ("Death and Youth," Concord, New Hampshire, 1929) and a monument to the First Division of the American Expeditionary Force ("Victory," 1924), which was a collaboration with architect Cass Gilbert. Their finished work was placed in President's Park, Washington, D.C. Both commissions were idealistic in their rendering and departed from the convincing realism of *The Minute Man* and Perkins statues.

THE MARQUIS DE LAFAYETTE (1883)

The Marquis de Lafayette by John Quincy Adams Ward is one of the most striking and memorable statues of the popular European hero of the Revolutionary War. A French aristocrat, Lafayette's support of the Colonists' cause was both financial and military. He served as a major general in the Continental Army under Washington, and his enthusiasm for the cause of liberty endeared him to the American people. Civic parks, streets, paintings, and statues are named in his honor in many American cities.

Erected on the green of the University of Vermont, Ward's statue of Lafayette was the gift of Burlington philanthropist John Purple Howard, whose financial contributions both to the city of Burlington and to the University of Vermont were considerable. He had stepped forward in 1881 to pay for the renovation of Old Mill, the principal building at UVM erected in the early nineteenth century, for which the cornerstone had been laid with great ceremony by the Marquis

Daniel Chester French, *The Minute Man*, 1873-75. Oblique view with pedestal dates. Photograph.

John Quincy Adams Ward, *The Marquis de Lafayette*, 1883. [Pedestal by Richard Morris Hunt] "The Gift of John P. Howard." Original site on the University Green in front of Old Mill. Postcard. "Burlington Vt. Lafayette Statue," Hugh Leighton and Co, Portland, Maine. #30297 .n.d. (Courtesy Special Collections, UVM)

de Lafayette on his triumphant return to and tour of the United States in 1824-1825. A Burlington native, Howard had achieved considerable financial success through the ownership, with his brother Daniel, of several hotels in New York City. His generosity in supporting the University of Vermont was matched by the charitable giving of his sister, Hannah Louisa Howard, to the city of Burlington. In *The 1881-'82 Biennial Report of the Trustees of the University of Vermont*, it was recorded that, "Mr. Howard, thoroughly appreciating the importance of having the institution [UVM] associated in the public mind with ideas of improvement and enterprise, determined to modernize the old building [Old Mill] without and within … the building when completed will be a noble monument to the generosity and public spirit of Mr. Howard."

The laying of the Old Mill cornerstone by Lafayette was but one of several "official acts" the Marquis had performed

John Hartley, *John Purple Howard*, 1883. Old Mill, UVM, Burlington, Vermont. "Gift of the Citizens of Burlington." Photograph.

while on his U.S. tour. He had earlier been present, in June 1825, at the cornerstone laying of Boston's Bunker Hill monument. An elaborate ceremony and extensive festivities accompanied Lafayette's visit to Burlington in July 1825, presided over by Governor C.P. Van Ness, the mayor of Burlington, and President-elect of the University Willard Preston. It was reported that Lafayette warmly greeted a large number of Revolutionary soldiers who were also present for the occasion. After a celebratory welcome and dinner, the triumphant Lafayette was led up the hill in a lengthy procession, accompanied by students of the University and by the citizens of Burlington—among them young John Purple Howard—to the University green, where he laid the cornerstone to the building now known as Old Mill. The students sang *"La Marseillaise,"* and later that evening, the Marquis was led by torchlight to the Burlington waterfront where he embarked on the *Phoenix* for Whitehall, New York.

Lafayette's visit to Burlington made a lasting impression upon John Purple Howard. Fifty years later, an older and now reflective Howard recalled this historic event. Inspired by the Centennial spirit, he felt it necessary to remind the members of the University community and the citizens of Burlington of Lafayette's role—both in the American Revolution and in the University's history. Howard proposed to honor Lafayette by commissioning a life-size ("heroic size") bronze statue of the distinguished patriot, designed by the celebrated American sculptor, John Quincy Adams Ward.

Howard's choice of Ward to take on the Lafayette project was most likely influenced by his familiarity with and probable involvement with the New York Chamber of Commerce—owing to his successful hotel business in the city. The Chamber had commissioned the sculptor to model a life-size statue of George Washington as first president of the United States. The finished work was to be placed on the spot where Washington took the oath of office (now Federal Hall at the junction of Wall and Broad streets). The NYCC *Washington* is a work closely related in stance and pose to the University's *Lafayette* on which Ward worked simultaneously[1].

---

1 Although Ward's New York City Washington wasn't completed and unveiled until November of 1883, his earlier

Ward's completed statue of the Marquis de Lafayette was placed on the University green with Old Mill in the background behind the statue. A portrait bust of benefactor John Purple Howard by sculptor John Hartley was placed in the niche of the center pavilion of Old Mill, thus aligning Lafayette, Howard, and the building in a logical visual narrative. As *The 1883-'84 Biennial Report of Trustees of the University of Vermont* recorded that the dedication of the statue was, "The occasion of one of the most imposing ceremonies ever witnessed in Vermont. It is estimated that fully ten thousand persons were present including a large number of the leading men of the State and of the neighboring States and Canada ... the statue is everyway worthy of the occasion and of this distinguished man who it commemorates. It is pronounced by the most competent judges to be not only the foremost work of ... J.Q.A. Ward ... but one of the very few successful works of art in bronze." Ward's statue was completed at the then considerable sum of $25,000 and unveiled June 26, 1883. It depicts a life-size, standing representation of Lafayette on a pedestal designed by noted architect Richard Morris Hunt with an appropriate *fleur-de-lis* motif carved in the frieze above the letters LA-FAYETTE. Much interest was noted in Hunt's pedestal when it was first placed in position in the fall of 1882. The *Burlington Free Press* observed on November 24, 1882, that it was made of "Barre granite, and is one of the handsomest pieces of stonework we have ever seen. It is in five pieces, base, plinth, die, frieze and cap and stands nine feet high." Seven months later, both Ward and Hunt attended the impressive ceremonies in Burlington held for the unveiling of the statue.

Ward's rendering of Lafayette was indebted to a number of sources. The *Burlington Free Press* of July 7,1882, noted that Ward discovered at George Washington's home at Mt. Vernon a "hitherto unknown head of Lafayette by David d'Anger[s]." D'Angers was a French sculptor who had struck two bas-relief medallions of Washington in 1830-'31 and whose full-length bronze statue of Washington, commissioned by Uriah Phillips Levy—the first Jewish commodore of the U.S. Navy—in 1834, was later placed in the rotunda of the

John Quincy Adams Ward, *George Washington*, 1883. Federal Hall, Wall Street, NYC. Photograph. (Courtesy Optimun Px, Wikimedia Commons)

[1878] Newburyport, Massachusetts, Washington commissioned by local citizen Daniel Tenny was well known and highly regarded. It depicted Washington in military dress as commander in chief of the continental army.

Jean-Antoine Houdon, *George Washington*, 1782-85. Virginia State Capital, Richmond, Virginia. Photograph. (Courtesy Ser Amanto di Nicolao, Wikimedia Commons)

Capitol. This "hitherto unknown head" was "the basis of his likeness of the Marquis for the statue which he is executing by the order of Mr. Howard for the University of Vermont."

Two additional sources were most likely the life-size standing statue of George Washington executed (1785/91) by the eighteenth-century French sculptor Jean-Antoine Houdon, and Ary Schaeffer's full-length oil painting of Lafayette dated 1824 and presented to the U.S. House of Representatives. The statue was an impressive and iconic neo-classical work commissioned by the State of Virginia to be placed in the rotunda of the capital building designed by Thomas Jefferson in Richmond, Virginia. Houdon's *Washington* retells the story of the Roman citizen/soldier/patriot Cincinnatus, depicting Washington as the embodiment of that patriotic nobleman, and the plow at his feet inferring his return to agricultural pursuits after bearing arms to defend his country. Ward's statue of Lafayette strikes a similar but more informal pose. Schaeffer's painting hangs to the left of the Speaker's Rostrum in the House of Representatives and a matching full-length portrait of George Washington dated 1834 painted by John Vanderlyn hangs to the right. Schaeffer's image also inspired Ward's pose of the Marquis and his decision to include a walking stick as well.

In Ward's depiction, the Marquis is shown in formal period dress wearing a three-quarter-length coat looking slightly to his right, his right hand resting on his walking stick, his left hand cocked on his hip with his right foot forward—a convincing, life-like rendering of the noted dignitary and friend of Washington.

On the occasion of the centenary of the visit of Lafayette to Burlington and the University campus in June 1925, a living reenactment of those events of June 1825 was performed with great enthusiasm by students at the University. Sadly, by late 1925 the statue of Lafayette had been removed from its original site, shunted to the north side of the campus green to make way for Sherry Fry's statue of *Ira Allen*, the gift in 1921 of trustee Thomas Wilbur from Manchester, Vermont. In so doing, the visual narrative between the Lafayette statue and Old Mill with its portrait bust of John Purple Howard in the central niche was dramatically disrupted. Nobody seemed to notice.

Today, the Lafayette, his missing walking stick now replaced, remains sited at the north end of the University green, freed from the overgrown shrubbery that had partially concealed him, making the work almost invisible for nearly forty years. The patina of the statue has been restored, and the portrait bust of John Purple Howard has been recently returned to his niche with a refurbished pedestal in the central pavilion of Old Mill. If the statue of Lafayette could once again occupy the site for which it was originally designed, the visual narrative which gave logical and concrete expression to Howard's generous gift would once more be in place.

The *Minute Man* and *Lafayette* statues each were made possible by the generosity of specific individuals. It was the vision of two older men who felt strongly about the need to commemorate great historical figures associated with America's Revolutionary War that made the statues possible. Hubbard and Howard realized the significance of "marking the spot" at which important historical events had taken place—places sacred to the memory of individuals associated with the Revolutionary War and the founding of the United States. The works are also expressions of the widespread enthusiasm manifested by the centennial celebrations. How else does one explain the many monuments, memorials, and markers to the Revolutionary War erected in the decades of 1870s and 1880s, commissioned by private individuals, public subscription, or by some legislative means at a time when so many Civil War cemeteries, monuments, and battlefield memorials were yet to be realized?[2]

Sherry Fry, *Ira Allen*, 1921. UVM Green, Burlington, Vermont. Pedestal inscriptions: "Ira Allen. Founder of the State of Vermont and Founder of this University, 1791." "Gift of Thomas B. Wilbur of Vermont, 1921."

---

2   In Vermont alone, two additional monuments marking the Revolutionary War were raised. The monument to *Ethan Allen,* completed in the spring of 1873 and unveiled July 4 of that year at Burlington's Green Mount cemetery, was carved in Italy after designs by Peter Stephenson. It was commissioned by the State of Vermont in 1855. The dramatic eight-foot high rendering of Allen depicted in period Green Mountain Boys uniform shows Allen's left arm raised heavenward, invoking the aid of "The Great Jehovah" on whom he called when his forces took the British fort at Ticonderoga. Allen is in period dress atop a granite Doric column whose shaft measures forty-two feet. The statue is placed over the Allen family plot in Burlington, the column and statue functioning as commemorative monument, family memorial, and grave marker. Near Bennington, Vermont, a three hundred-foot high obelisk of rusticated stone known as the *Bennington Battle Monument* was dedicated in 1889, its initial conception conceived in the 1870s, although the battle was actually fought in nearby Walloomsac, New York.

John Quincy Adams Ward, *The Marquis de Lafayette*. 1883.
Photograph, before 1920. (Courtesy Special Collections, UVM)

John Quincy Adams Ward, *The Marquis de Lafayette*, 1883. Current
siting, North side of University Green, UVM, Burlington, Vermont.
Postcard. "Lafayette Statue. #21, Published by H.F. Perkins.
Burlington, VT" n.d. (Courtesy Special Collections, UVM)

John Quincy Adams Ward, *The Marquis de Lafayette*, 1883. Current siting. Photograph, 2015.

CHAPTER TWO

"With Jealous Care": Military Cemeteries at Home and Abroad

"We cannot dedicate, we cannot consecrate, we cannot hallow this ground. The brave men, living and dead, who struggled here, have consecrated it far above our poor power to add or detract. —Abraham Lincoln, 1863

"It is the duty of the Gov't to collect together and protect with jealous care the remains of those who have died in so noble a service." —Assistant Quartermaster General Edmund Whitman, 1869

"I have many times asked myself whether there can be more potent advocates of peace upon earth through the years to come than this massed multitude of silent witnesses to the desolation of war." —King George V, 1922

To WANDER THROUGH the 175 acres of lush and wooded tranquility of Mt. Auburn Cemetery in Cambridge, Massachusetts, is to understand the appeal of a "good death" to mid-century Americans. Mt. Auburn was the first of the so-called '"rural cemeteries" opened in 1831. To this day, it remains the most impressive expression of that movement. Here, one communes with the great and the anonymous, lovingly and individually buried. Here, you find the graves of such luminaries as Mary Baker Eddy, Isabelle Stewart Gardner, Felix Frankfurter, Oliver Wendell Homes, McGeorge Bundy, Curt Gowdy, and thousands of others.

Mt. Auburn is part arboretum, part sanctuary, part museum and wholly cemetery. A closer look at the graves reveals the final resting place of Charles Russell Lowell and a cenotaph of the family of Robert Gould Shaw. There is a monument to the dead of Boston Independent Corps of Cadets; there is the grave of Captain Nathaniel Bowditch. Near the chapel is an elephant-sized marble statue of a sphinx by sculptor Millard Milmore to commemorate the end of Civil War. One learns that among the 93,000 graves are over 1,000 that belong to Civil War veterans.

But the beauty of the place is deceptive. For individuals and for the nation, the possibility of a "good death" died on the battlefields of the Civil War—at Bull Run and at Shiloh, at Antietam and at Gettysburg, at Petersburg and at Andersonville. In the survivors' minds, the leaves and flowers and shade were replaced with the gore of blasted bone, gobbets of

Martin Milmore, *American Sphinx*, 1872. Mt. Auburn Cemetery.

Charles Russell Gravestone, Mt. Auburn Cemetery.

flesh, smashed faces, and bloated bodies.

This essay treats how two nations searched for, found, and buried avalanches of war dead unique in their histories. Given our American obsession (and the roughly $100 million spent yearly) to trace every MIA soldier in Vietnam from forty years ago, it is hard to imagine that in the American Civil War and World War I, nearly 50 percent of the dead were never even found.

In the beginning of each war, attention to the wounded and dead was haphazard and scattered. Only later did the governments devote significant resources to search and burial. Significantly, both the US and British governments came to similar conclusions: that, though death often came en masse, burials would be individual—rank in life would give way to comradeship in death; burial grounds would be havens of beauty and invitation, not sumps of abandoned decay; and, by and large, the dead would be buried roughly where they fell.

Burial party on the battlefield of Cold Harbor, Virginia. April,1865. Negative by John Reekie; print and caption by Alexander Gardner. (Library of Congress, Prints and Photographs Division, Civil War Photographs)

An Avalanche of Death

By the end of the Civil War, an estimated 650,000 Union and Confederate soldiers would be dead, almost two per-cent of the population. (For today's population, that would equal roughly six million deaths.) This figure represents more fatalities than resulted from the Revolutionary War, the War of 1812, the Spanish American War, World Wars I and II, and the Korean War—*combined*. Soldiers were blown apart, scattered across fields, left to rot. After the heat of battle, they were often thrown indiscriminately into trenches. They were doubly destroyed: first by shell-fire, then by weather, vandalism, or wild animals.

There were no preparations for such casualties. There was no grave registration, no identification system for individual soldiers, no dog tags, no ambulance service, no system for informing relatives of the soldier's death, no storage of coffins, no protocol for burying the dead, no national cemeteries.

In September 1861, a desperate War Department issued General Order 75, which made all commanders responsible for burying their dead as close as possible to the battlefield and, for sanitation's sake, as soon as possible. The order also required that a headboard with the solder's name be placed on the grave. But wooden boards and chalk markings did not last long. Often, solders were in retreat. Always, the surviving soldiers were exhausted or wounded. Burials were hasty, at

Alexandria National Cemetery, 1876.

Cyprus Hills National Cemetery, Brooklyn, New York.

best. But it was the first time anywhere in the world that such an order was promulgated.

The next year, following the bloody battles of Peninsular Campaign, Second Bull Run and particularly Shiloh, Congress gave the President power to purchase cemetery grounds, and "cause them to be securely enclosed, to be used as a national cemetery for the soldiers who shall die in the service of the country." This established the goal that all the war dead should be honorably buried at government expense.

In 1862, the government created twelve new cemeteries by purchasing land for cemeteries near battlefields, troop concentration points, hospitals, or existing civilian cemeteries. The beginning of a national cemetery system therefore occurred at cities like Brooklyn, New York; Annapolis, Maryland; and Springfield, Illinois. However, despite Congress' bold legislative statement, the construction of cemeteries throughout the war could only be described as piecemeal.

EARLY NATIONAL CEMETERIES

Given 6,000 soldiers killed in action and 21,000 more casualties from both sides of the battle of Gettysburg, it is clear why Pennsylvania Governor Andrew G. Curtain rushed in to help local residents establish a permanent gravesite. Curtain solicited funds from the eighteen Northern states whose troops had fought there. Pennsylvania then bought seventeen acres on the northwest slope of the now-sacred Cemetery Hill. William Saunders, the superintendent of the experimental

Graves of Unknown near the Soldiers National Monument at Gettysburg Cemetery.

Randolph Rogers, *Soldiers National Monument*,1869. Gettysburg National Cemetery.

gardens of the newly created Department of Agriculture in Washington, DC, was brought in to design the grounds.

Saunders designed a central Soldiers' National Monument, around which the graves were laid out, state by state, in great semi-circles. "The prevailing expression of the cemetery," said Saunders, "should be that of simple grandeur." All the graves were considered equal—officers and men, states large and small. Bodies were still being dug up and re-interred when President Lincoln gave his celebrated dedicatory address.

A year later, the state of Maryland moved to establish a state cemetery where some 22,000 troops were killed, wounded, or went missing at the Battle of Antietam in 1862. At first, officials planned to bury soldiers from both sides, but residual bitterness over the war persuaded the state to reverse course. Consequently, only Union dead are interred here. Burials were by state. Officers were buried in distinct plots, as were unknown US soldiers.

Today, we think of Arlington National Cemetery in Virginia as a kind of American Valhalla for our heroic war dead. In fact, it was founded in May 1864, when Quartermaster General Montgomery C. Meigs ordered a search for a site to establish a large new national military cemetery in the Washington area. Of the suggested sites, Meigs was most attracted to the Arlington estate belonging to the family of General Robert E. Lee. The property was high and free from floods that

Carl Conrads, *The Private Soldier Monument*, 1876. Antietam Cemetery.

Quartermaster General Montgomery C. Meigs. Jefferson Barracks Military Post, MO.

might unearth graves, and it had a magnificent view of the District of Columbia. Meigs' decision to use the Lee estate was also highly personal. The Quartermaster General was bitter over the death of his officer son in Western Virginia, which he claimed was murder by the young man's Southern captors. To make the Arlington property a national cemetery would forever prevent the return of Lee and his family. Meigs himself was later buried within 100 yards of Arlington House, along with his wife and *son*.

In the western theater of war, Union generals created three cemeteries near specific battle sites: Stones River, Knoxville, and Chattanooga. The most prominent of them was at Chattanooga. On December 25, 1863, Major General George H. Thomas issued General Orders No. 296, creating a national cemetery in commemoration of the Battles of Missionary Ridge, Lookout Mountain, and Chickamauga. Thomas advanced the burial mission one step further when he ordered that the cemetery would receive "all who should *hereafter* [emphasis added] fall in that region defending their country." After the war, this injunction to bury all veterans would become national policy. Thomas selected approximately seventy-five acres of a round hill that faced Missionary Ridge on one side and Lookout Mountain on the other. When asked by a chaplain if he wanted troops buried by state as had been done at Gettysburg, Thomas reportedly replied, "No, no. Mix them all up. I'm sick of state's rights."

John Rogers Meigs Tomb. Arlington National Cemetery.

Montgomery Meigs Tomb. Arlington National Cemetery.

PRIVATE RE-PATRIATION EFFORTS

Some relatives with means went to the South (or paid an agent to go on their behalf) to look for their fallen loved ones and bring them home to a family plot or a local cemetery. They paid for the zinc lined caskets, the embalming, and the freight costs to get their sons and brothers home. For the great majority of families, however, such treatment was too complicated and too expensive.

A story told by Frances Wadhams Davenport Ormsbee of Vermont shows how arduous these journeys could be. Thirty years after the Civil War ended, Ms. Ormsbee recounted her trip to Virginia from Vermont to retrieve the bodies of her first husband, George Daniel Davenport, and his close friend Charles J. Ormsbee. Both had joined the Union forces in the spring of 1861 in Brandon, Vermont. Both were mortally wounded May 5, 1864, in the Second Battle of the Wilderness in Virginia. Both men had been hastily buried in makeshift graves close to where they had fallen, their names and regiment scrawled in pencil on temporary wooden markers.

Not until the War ended a year later was Frances able to safely travel to retrieve her husband's and Ormsbee's remains. To do so required many requests from the Sanitary Commission and US Army, as well as directions to the gravesites in Virginia. Frances and several of her brothers traveled first to Washington, DC, and on to Fredericksburg where they purchased caskets. There, they were aided by a hospital steward from Pennsylvania who directed them to the site where the men had been buried in shallow graves—part of a row of twelve in the middle of a cornfield.

Frances and her brothers hired two Negro men to exhume the bodies. Her brothers urged the widow to remain away

Unknown photographer, *George D. Davenport and his wife Francis Wadhams Davenport*, 1860. Tintype. Courtesy, Emily Wadhams

Davenport Grave. Pine Hill Cemetery, Brandon, Vermont.

from the gravesites so as not to be overwhelmed by the sight and smell of the bodies. The clothing of the men had begun to deteriorate, but Frances immediately recognized the cloth and the buttons she had used to make the shirt her husband was wearing. Both men's bodies were placed in caskets purchased for the trip back to Vermont. Frances would later marry Ormsbee's brother, who became governor of Vermont in the 1890s.

A Concentrated Search

By war's end, with only about 100,000 registered burials (less than one third of the estimated Union dead in the war), the Northern Army Quartermaster Department launched its own campaign to search for, recover, identify, and bury as many soldiers' remains as possible. In January 1866, Assistant Quartermaster Edmund Whitman send out a circular to over 300 newspapers in the country asking army chaplains and surgeons for information on the whereabouts of soldier burials. In it, Whitman promised "all that human care and industry can accomplish" in this mission, but he had to acknowledge that "...it is evident that the sad information 'unknown' will meet many an anxious inquiring eye."

The Quartermaster's office received thousands of replies from families, friends and comrades—often with exact loca-

Clara Barton raising the flag at Andersonville
National Cemetery, Georgia, August 17, 1865.
(*Harpers Weekly* October 7, 1865)

tions. For the next five years, they sent teams of soldiers to survey "every battlefield, burial ground, field and general hospital, public and private burial place, encampment, bivouac, picket station, outpost, port of embarkation or landing, field, garden, wood, roadside and prison."[3]   They found bodies in individual, group and mass graves. Identification, if possible, was obtained through letters, receipts, diaries, or photographs found on the bodies; by marks on belts or cartridge boxes; and by interviews with relatives and survivors found through additional public circulars.

On this "harvest of death," Whitman himself seems to have traveled over 30,000 miles. At each battlefield, Whitman and his men had to study the topography and the course of the fighting in "rocks and ravines, the woods and groves, mountains, swamps, canebrakes and routes," looking for grave markers. To every person they met, white and African-American, they asked the same question: "Do you know of any graves of Union soldiers in your neighborhood?" Changes in the landscape made geographical identification difficult. Time, weather, hasty burials, and imperfect memories were their passive obstructions. Willful desecration and deceitful information were their growing enemies.

As Southern resistance to the project grew (although some individual Southerners were helpful), pressure mounted to protect the work in progress. In 1867, Congress passed the "Act to Establish and Protect National Cemeteries." According to the legislation, the secretary of war was designated to purchase land as necessary and build the enclosures, with each grave to be marked with a small headstone, name, rank, company, regiments, and date of death. The act also declared that

---

3 "Report on National Cemeteries and Mortuary Records," by BVT. Lt. Col. E.M. Whitman, A.Q.M. May 10, 1869.

any willful destruction, mutilation, defacement, or removal of gravestones or other structures would be a misdemeanor. The cemetery superintendent was empowered to arrest any culprits and bring them before a federal magistrate.

As for the cemeteries themselves, Assistant Quartermaster Whitman's promise to honor the "noble martyrs in a just and holy cause" led him to describe four principles to govern the selection and development of the burial grounds. These would include: localities of historical interest, convenient access, placement on the great thoroughfares of the nation, and places presenting favorable conditions for ornamentation and commemoration.

Quartermaster General Meigs laid out a general plan, which included a lodge for each cemetery's superintendent—invariably a veteran. The lodge was in the French Second Empire style with a mansard roof and brick or stone walls surrounding the premises. Other features included rostrums for speakers on memorial days and a variety of ornamentation, such as piles of cannon balls, obelisks, and an inverted cannon—which at Antietam marked the resting place of no fewer than six generals, three on each side.

The cemeteries varied greatly. Some, like the one in Marietta, Georgia, had elaborate gates. Almost all had graves arranged around a flagpole. Architects developed different geometric designs for the stones: squares, rectangles, a half-wheel, even a compass-rose pattern. There were lots of plantings of larger leafy trees to ward off the hot Southern sun. Each of the cemeteries, regardless of individual designs, bade the visitor to pause and honor (in Whitman's words), "the heroic sacrifice, [and] to teach to succeeding generations lessons of undying patriotism."

By 1870, the number of national cemeteries was seventy-three, and these were located at battlefields, former prisons, field hospitals, and garrisons. The number of remains interred in national cemeteries, private plots, and post cemeteries, together with those marked for re-internment, totaled 315,555. This final figure was only 26,175 fewer than the total number of Union death as estimated in 1866. Of the total buried by 1870, there were 173,109 positive identifications and 143,446 unknown remains. In other words, 58 percent of the recovered dead were identified.[4] In a few cases the "unknowns" were buried in separate sections of cemeteries, such as at Antietam, but ultimately they were co-mingled with the named dead.

There never was a formal category of the missing. According to historian Sara Leach, "We are not sure the [Quartermaster General's] office ever acknowledged that soldiers were missing, per se. We do not think there was any comprehensive effort to account for everyone who served the Union. Sometimes the 'missing' had simply walked away because they were fed up or needed to return home to plow fields, keep a business running, care for sick family members, etc." The [Quartermaster General's] goal was to honorably inter all the dead that could be located.[5]

In 1870, Meigs asked the noted landscape architect Frederick Law Olmsted to help design the plantings at the national cemeteries. Olmsted, as executive secretary of the US Sanitary Commission, had a firsthand awareness of the sufferings

---

4 Edward Steere. "The Evolution of the National Cemetery System 1865-1880." *Quartermaster Review*. Quartermaster Foundation. May/June 1953. Web. 3 August 2013.

5 Letter to the authors.

of the troops. The Commission was a private relief agency sanctioned by federal legislation to support sick and wounded US Army soldiers. Olmsted recommended that cemetery designs "establish permanent dignity and tranquility… sacredness and protection being expressed in the enclosing wall and in the perfect tranquility of the trees within." Several years later, Meigs would issue his "Instructions Relative to the Cultivation and Care of Trees in the National Cemeteries." [6]

But the central feature of all the cemeteries—the main act, of course—was the graves. Row upon row of them, up and down, over hillock and hollow—white marble stones of exactly the same height, like dominos ready to fall. It was lost on few veterans that the regular rows of headstones resembled an Army encampment. To many veterans, this configuration immediately evoked the "Bivouac of the Dead," a poem from the Mexican-American War by Theodore O'Hara, which became popular in both the North and South. Quartermaster General Meigs himself had verses from the poem installed on the entrance to Arlington Cemetery.[7]

> The muffled drum's sad roll has beat
> The soldier's last tattoo;
> No more on life's parade shall meet
> That brave and fallen few.
> On Fame's eternal camping-ground
> Their silent tents are spread,
> And Glory guards, with solemn round,
> The bivouac of the dead.

Also, Meigs determined that every known dead soldier would be honored by name. In typically blunt language he wrote:

> I do not believe that those who visit the graves of their relatives would have any satisfaction in finding them ticketed and numbered like London Policemen or convicts...The whole object is to gratify a sentiment; and I think there can be no doubt that the mere numbering of the dead would shock 99 out of 100 visitors, while all would be gratified to find the graves of their dead friends distinguished by inscriptions giving name and rank, date and Regiment, which last also gives the state from which he entered the service.[8]

---

6 Sara Amy Leach. "Designing the First National Cemeteries: National Park Service." *Nps.gov.* National Parks Service. Web. 3 August 2013.

7 In fall 2001, the National Cemetery Administration commenced an initiative to install a new cast-aluminum tablet featuring the first stanza of "Bivouac of the Dead" in all the existing national cemeteries where they are missing, as well as national cemeteries under development.

8 National Archives and Records Administration, RG92 E225, Box 787, Headstones, Meigs to Secretary of War William Belknap, July 8, 1879.

Two controversies, one aesthetic and one momentous, arose at the end of what Whitman called a "harvest of death." Both involved Quartermaster General Meigs. The first was Meigs' determination to have metal headstones, painted with a rust-resistant covering. Congress, however, decided that marble was the better material. In the second case, Meigs argued that the national cemeteries under construction should only contain bodies of those killed in the war. The Army, however, with urging from veterans, overruled him. They were doubtless moved by the blunt statement of General William T. Sherman: "Surely, when practicable these cemeteries should be devoted to the burial of soldiers for all time to come."

On March 3, 1873, Congress appropriated a million dollars to replace the headboards with markers of "durable stone" and allowed the secretary of war to determine "the size and model for such headstones, and the standards of quality, and color of the stone to be used." The face would display a sunken shield carrying the number of the grave, rank, name of soldier, and the name of home state. For some unknown soldiers, a block six inches square by thirty inches long would bear only the grave number. Other unidentified bodies were buried beneath the common headstones and designated simply "Unknown US Soldier." In the cemeteries that contained Confederate dead, their pointed gravestone of roughly the same size would the name, state, and "C.S.A."

In her critically acclaimed book about death and the Civil War, *This Republic of Suffering,* historian Drew Gilpin Faust called this American grave-building program the largest national public works program in American history to that time.[9]

A British "Empire of the Dead"

Half a century later, World War I forced the British Empire to endure a similar four-year deluge of battlefield deaths. As far as we can tell, the British never studied the American precedent for collecting and burying unheard-of numbers of war dead, although the English poet and veteran of the trenches Edmund Blunden points out that American Civil War "called fresh attention and imagination forth on the subject" of the proper treatment of the war dead.[10] What gave urgency to the British task was the staggering number of bodies. World War I necessitated the largest volunteer army ever assembled by Great Britain, and the fighting was exceedingly close—shelling on the Somme front was occasionally audible across the English Channel.

British military burial policy had begun to change during the Boer War (1899-1902), when almost 25,000 Empire troops died of wounds and disease. Before that, mass graves were the rule, but after the Boer, the Empire began to place bodies in individual graves in some 365 cemeteries throughout the colony. Their maintenance, however, was poor.

A short decade later, identification of the scores of fallen was difficult or impossible. Almost half of the British World War I dead was simply missing. "Many graves were frequently under fire and inaccessible … not only have a large number

---

9   Drew Gilpin Faust. *This Republic of Suffering: Death and the American Civil War.* New York: Vintage. 2009. p. 219.

10   Edmund Blunden. "Introduction." *The Unending Vigil* by Philip Longworth. Barnsley: Pen & Sword Military. 2010.

Gravestones of Union and Confederate Dead. Cyprus Hills National Cemetery, Brooklyn, New York.

Fabian Ware. Commonwealth War Graves Commission. Undated photograph.

of bodies been destroyed beyond all recognition by the enemy's artillery fire before burial but that all traces of graves themselves have in a large number of cases been obliterated."[11] Many dead were, of course, in no-man's land, which made retrieving them doubly dangerous, and an untold number of soldiers were killed in trying to recover the bodies of dead comrades.

The dominant figure in the effort to collect and bury the Empire's World War I dead was Fabian Ware, a journalist and former schools inspector who, overwhelmed by the carnage, volunteered to head up a Red Cross rescue unit. Too old to fight, Ware nevertheless had immense energy and powers of persuasion. Having lived in France for a number of years, he was fluent with both the language and manners of the French. He was also a natural diplomat.

Ware's Red Cross work was first to bring the wounded to aid stations. But his prime interest shifted to the hundreds and thousands of bodies that were accumulating on the Western front. He told his Red Cross team to make careful note of where the dead were buried and the state of those graves. He knew that as soon as possible, families of the slain would wish to visit those graves, and he wanted them in a suitable state. Without suitable care for the graves, what would greet them?

---

11   Julie Summers, *British Commonwealth and War Cemeteries.* Oxford: Shire Publications. 2010. p. 19

Burial detail washing their hands in shell hole.
Bawtree Collection, Commonwealth War
Graves Commission. Undated photograph.

"Intolerable ruins, the rusted wire, the wasted ground, cemeteries smashed by shellfire, [and] drunkenly leaning crosses." [12]

In contrast to the Quartermaster General's experience in the American South, Ware and the Red Cross met no civilian interference while searching for bodies. In fact, French and Belgian citizens, including children, often aided search parties. Any "vandalism" came from repeated shellings in no-man's land and elsewhere, so that some bodies were buried two or even three times.

As early as October 1914, Ware persuaded his superiors to put up temporary crosses and then methodically mark the graves of the dead as each battle ended. Once it was decided to bury all abroad, it became imperative to Ware and others that the heavy loss felt by surviving loved ones should be assuaged as much as possible. Photographers were employed to take photographs of individual graves in France and Belgium and to furnish the photos "to relatives on application, free of cost." [13]

Ware's diplomacy and fluent French were instrumental in reaching agreements with French and Belgian governments

---

12   Herbert Fairlie Wood and John Swettenham. *Silent Witnesses.* Toronto: A.M. Hakkert, Ltd. 1974. p. 8.

13   Fabian Ware. "The Registration and Care of Graves." January 23, 1917.

Collecting an identification disc from a fallen hero, **August 12, 1918.** Imperial War Museum (Photo #Q. 3963)

Burying Canadian Dead May 1918. National Archives of Canada (PA 4352). Undated photograph.

to acquire land for the cemeteries. The grateful French gave the British the land for the cemeteries, but wanted to restrict the size in order to get more land back into the hands of its farmers. Wares' Red Cross unit gained official recognition in 1915 and material support in terms of reactions, billets, and titles.

Eventually, however, the task was so immense that the Red Cross could no longer manage it. What was called for was a wholly new quasi-governmental arm with a specific focus on burial of the dead. With the war now definitely worldwide, and with hundreds of thousands of Empire troops in combat, the new commission was named the Imperial War Graves Commission. The Prince of Wales was the president. With Ware as chairman, other members included Rudyard Kipling and Sir William Garstin, the architect of the first Aswan Dam. Both of these men had already lost sons in the war.

In its enabling legislation, the Commission was charged with caring for the members of the Armed Forces of the British Empire who had "died of wounds inflicted, accident occurring or disease contracted, while on active service whether on sea or land." Its powers included the acquisition of land for cemeteries and permanent memorials, the burials themselves, keeping records of the graves and tending the graves both inside and outside formal war cemeteries. The Commission was also mandated to individually commemorate each soldier who had no known grave, which amounted to an estimated 315,000 in France and Belgium alone. Simply put, the Commission had a dual mission—to honor the dead and to comfort the living.

Canadian Graves being decorated by Nursing Sisters June 30, 1918. Commonwealth War Graves Commission. Undated photograph.

Laborious and detailed work carving the headstones. Commonwealth War Graves Commission. Undated photograph.

THE WORK OF THE COMMISSION

From its first meeting, the Commission committed itself to a momentous democratization of death—there would be no distinction between officers and men, between creed and nationality. In answer to several heated demands for special treatment for officers, Ware wrote, "The one point of view that seems to me to be often overlooked in this matter is that of the officers themselves, who in ninety-nine cases out of a hundred will tell you that if they are killed they would wish to be among their men."[14]

Recognition would come in the form of uniform headstones over the graves for each body, placed in cemeteries created close to or directly upon the places of battle where the soldiers had died. Just as military-issue dress and uniform—from haircuts to battle gear—was designed to eliminate individual differences between soldiers, so too the "uniform" treatment of headstones echoed that common experience of death. As Colonel Henry Osborne later explained in his 1929 speech to the Empire Club of Canada, "The headstones are meant to typify the union of all [soldiers] in 'motive, action and in

14   Summers, p. 17.

A Soldier in the Great War gravestone. Thiepval Monument to the Missing in the distance.

Gravestones of officers and enlisted men side by side. Thiepval, France. Commonwealth War Graves Commission Cemetery

death.' By their very uniformity, they speak in one voice of one death, one sacrifice, for a cause that was common to all."[15]

Even though most of the temporary graves were designated with a cross, the Commission decided against that for the final design. A plain stone allowed for recognition of different faiths. The cruciform shape could not contain the information desired. But the decisive argument came down to money. To manufacture and ship metal crosses to the cemeteries would cost 20-30 percent more. Every grave was marked with a headstone of Portland stone two feet six inches high, one foot three inches wide, and three inches thick and slightly curved at the top the better to withstand the weather. On its face, inscribed above an appropriate religious symbol and in letters designed by MacDonald Gill, were carved the regimental badge, rank, name, unit, date of death and age of each casualty. The rows of headstones would give the appearance of a battalion on parade, thus repeating the "bivouac of the dead" theme from the American Civil War.

Most headstones are inscribed with a cross or a Star of David, except for those deceased known to be atheist or non-Christian. Since many headstones were for unidentified casualties, the Commission, led by Kipling, developed the following epitaph: "A SOLDIER OF THE GREAT WAR, KNOWN UNTO GOD."

Importantly, the Commission decided not to allow private physical memorials, but it did permit some individualistic verbal farewells, limited to sixty-five characters. At Ypres Reserve Cemetery in Belgium and Bunyans Cemetery in France,

---

15   Col. Henry Osborne, "The Great Remembrance," a speech before The Empire Club of Canada. Toronto, Canada, 14 February 1929.

examples include both secular and religious sentiments:

"That we might live."
"Peace after strife."
"Not forgotten."
"Greater love hath no man than this."
"Blessed are the pure in heart, for they shall see God."
"Will meet you in the Great Beyond."
"The path of duty was the way to glory."
"On his Soul Sweet Jesus Have Mercy."

A second momentous decision by the Commission was not to permit repatriation of the dead. This was both for reasons of expense and because such a policy would create a *de facto* economic class system between families with means and those without. Such a prohibition, however, meant that the authorities worked hard to provide families with photographs of the gravesites and to help them visit in person.

The cemeteries' design came under the supervision of master architects officially appointed by the Commission early in 1918, while the war was still underway. The principal architects were Sir Edward Lutyens, Reginald Blomfield, and Sir Herbert Baker. Under them were a number of junior architects, most of who had fought in the war. Strong disagreements between some of the architects caused Ware decided to hire an arbiter—Sir Frederic Kenyon, director of the British Museum—who was acceptable to the various parties.

The Commission determined that the "quiet resting place," the English rural parish church cemetery with its enclosure and thoughtful landscaping (mown grass, appropriate flowering shrubs, etc.) would be more than a metaphor. Such a layout would be the most powerful form of individual and collective commemoration because it was the most familiar and the most clearly understood. As early as 1916, in the depths of the war, a team of gardeners from Kew Gardens in London went out to give advice about trees and shrubs. A member of the team, Arthur Hill, said that the plantings would "help to cheer our men who are constant visitors to our cemeteries and who frequently pass their cemeteries when on the march." As Frederic Kenyon would write in his 1918 Report: "There is no reason why cemeteries should be places of gloom; but the restfulness of grass and the brightness of flowers in fitting combination would appear to strike the proper note of brightness and life."[16] Special recognition was given to the Dominion armies by planting "trees indigenous to the countries that came to the defense of the Empire. The Canadians, for example, would receive maple trees and the Austra-

---

16   Sir Frederic Kenyon. *War Graves: How the Cemeteries Abroad Will Be Designed.* London: HMSO. 1918. p. 13.

Sir Edwin Lutyens, *Stone of Remembrance*. Sir Reginald Blomfield, *Cross of Sacrifice*. Tyne Cot Cemetery, Passchendaele, Belgium.

lians seedlings of Tasmanian eucalyptus trees."[17]

The cost of preparing and maintaining this vast collection of Imperial gravesites would be borne according to the homes of the dead. Thus, about 80 percent of the money would come from Great Britain and the remaining 20 percent from the Dominions. Wherever possible, the Dominions agreed, British labor and British stone would be used.

MONUMENTS WITHIN THE CEMETERIES

In addition to the graves with their identical stones and symbolic plantings, each cemetery was to have what Kenyon called a central monument: "Simple durable, dignified and expressive of the higher feelings with which we regard our dead." Kenyon's final report recommended that two styles of monument should be erected in each cemetery. A Memorial Stone, designed by Lutyens, was to be placed on the east side of the cemetery with the graves facing it, if possible. Lutyens described the Memorial Stone as "one great fair stone of fine proportions, 12 feet in length, lying raised upon three steps, of which the first and the third shall be twice the width of the second ... each stone shall bear, in indelible lettering, some fine thought or words of sacred dedication.[18] For dedicatory language on the Stone of Remembrance, as it came to be

---

17   Captain A.W. Hill. "Our Soldiers' Graves." *Journal of the Royal Horticultural Society* Vol. XLV., Part I, 1919, p. 8)

18   Kenyon, p. 6.

American graves. Aisne-Marne American Cemetery near Belleau, France.

known, Rudyard Kipling had gone to the Bible, "For this being the one Book, which was beyond criticism." From the fourth chapter of Ecclesiastics, he chose the line "Their name liveth for evermore."

Probably cautious after the debate over crosses as headstones, Kenyon's second central monument would directly convey the "Christian character" and the "idea of self-sacrifice" of those who had died. "I have no doubt that great distress would be felt if our cemeteries lack this recognition of the fact that we are a Christian Empire," he observed. This Empire was Christian in part only, because as Kenyon had to acknowledge, the Muslim and Hindu soldiers were to be buried apart. As for others: "the Jews are necessarily intermixed with their Christian comrades; but it is believed that their feelings will be satisfied by the inclusion of their religious symbol [the Star of David] in the design of their headstones."[19] Kenyon's recommendation therefore, was for the erection of a cross of some sort to also be place in the cemeteries. The final form of the Cross of Sacrifice was the work of Blomfield. A bronze longsword, blade down, is embedded on the face of the cross. The Cross's symbolism is unmistakably Christian. Its multi-tiered octagonal base also suggested Celtic roadside crosses.

Together, the Cross and the Stone immediately established a visual frame of reference and became the identifying symbols of these military cemeteries. In any cemetery with more than forty graves, a Cross of Sacrifice was placed. Where there were more than a thousand, the cemetery would include one of Lutyens' Stones. While the size of Lutyens' Great

---

19   Kenyon, p. 6.

Stone remained constant, Blomfield's Cross varied depending upon the scale of the cemetery. The Cross came in four sizes: fourteen-and-a-half, twenty, twenty-four, and thirty feet in height.

During the heat of battle, some soldiers were buried on the spot. A number of cemeteries were built during the fighting and remained undisturbed through the war. But others were torn up by renewed fighting even several times. At the end of the war, there were an estimated 150,000 individual or group graves spread along the Ypres and Somme battlefronts that could not be left there due to the French and Belgian desire to have their agricultural land back in production. Therefore, a concentrated search went on for two years after the Armistice, much like that after the American Civil War, in which the Army systematically combed the countryside and eventually recovered over 200,000 bodies, which were assembled into designated cemeteries as near as possible to where they fell.

CONNECTIONS AND CONCLUSIONS

One of the most striking revelations of writing this chapter is that there is no evidence that anyone from the Imperial War Graves Commission looked at the American experience in the Civil War. In effect, the British reinvented the wheel when it came to dealing with the carnage of war. Still, the similarities outnumber the differences. Both governments had similar challenges in finding, identifying, and burying enormous numbers of the dead and somehow accounting for the missing. Both had to balance design, aesthetics, and cost. Neither had unlimited space in which to build—the Americans because of vandalism in a still hostile South, the British because French and Belgian farmers wanted to put as much land back into cultivation after four years of war.

Technological advances that greatly speeded the process of carving through the use of sandblasting and pantograph machines aided both projects, and this allowed both institutions to come up with similar designs in the layouts and in the gravestones. Both countries came up with relatively similar stones and uniformity of message.

In the American cemeteries, men and officers were often buried side by side. While one might expect this in the more egalitarian American society, the fact that the more rigid British society rejected such stratification was a testament to the Commission's commitment to democracy in death. This same British "caste society" prohibited any family from bringing home their dead sons—either at private or public expense. Surely, cost played a role in this decision, but the more forceful factor was an extension of the doctrine of comradeship in death.[20]

---

20   In this way, the American World War I burial practices differed from those of the British. The Americans agreed to repatriate the dead at the families' requests. Seventy percent asked for such action. And the American Battle Monuments Commission, at the urging of the Gold Star Mothers organization, chose marble crosses as headstones.

CHAPTER THREE

The Missing and the Unknown Memorialized

"The work of death was Civil War America's most fundamental and most demanding undertaking."—Drew Gilpin Faust

"Remembrance is part of the landscape. Anyone who walks through northern France or Flanders will find traces of the terrible, almost unimaginable human losses of the war, and of efforts to commemorate the fallen."—Jay Winter

"Nothing is truly mine except my name. I only borrowed this dust."—Passing Through, Stanley Kunitz

IT IS ESTIMATED that 850,000 soldiers were killed in the American Civil War. Almost half of those soldiers were never identified or were simply unaccounted for. It was Clara Barton—the "Angel of the Battlefield," director of the American Red Cross, and founder of the Office of Missing Soldiers—who tirelessly responded to enquiries and provided information to families of more than 20,000 soldiers missing at War's end. How to commemorate those missing and unknown commensurate with the known dead was a question raised by those who believed in the democracy of death.

Similarly, of the estimated one million soldiers who died in World War I fighting for the British Empire, close to a third or more were never found or identified. The scale of death created unexpected and enormous difficulties. "Missing," "disappeared," and "unknown," have a dark and unsettling ring to them. They cannot accurately describe the violent and sinister forces that obliterated discernable traces of identification of soldiers killed in battle. Where there were no bodily remains, there were no graves. The commemoration of soldiers whose bodily remains could not be found presented a different set of problems than those whose remains would be interred either in newly created military cemeteries or, in rare cases, family plots.

Common to both the American Civil War and World War I was a policy based upon democratic principles: a policy that sought an honorable burial of the dead, whether known, unknown, or missing. In both wars, the cost of commemoration for a common soldier or officer was borne by the respective governments. As historian Drew Gilpin Faust has noted, such an undertaking marked the first "public project" undertaken by the US government.

Montgomery Meigs, *Civil War Unknowns Memorial,* 1866. Arlington National Cemetery.

A memorial to unknown Civil War soldiers whose remains were not identified was unveiled in the newly created Arlington National Cemetery in 1866. Designed by Quartermaster General Montgomery C. Meigs, *The Civil War Unknowns Monument* is both memorial and grave—a memorial structure placed over a burial chamber containing the unidentified remains of more than 2,000 Union and Confederate dead gathered from nearby battlefields and skirmishes. Six feet in height, twelve feet long, and four feet wide, the granite memorial bears an inscription that reads:

> Beneath this stone repose the bones of two thousand one hundred and eleven unknown soldiers gathered after the war. From the fields of Bull Run and the route to the Rappahannock, their remains could not be identified. But their names and deaths are recorded in the archives of their country. And its grateful citizens honor them as of their noble army of martyrs. May they rest in peace. September A.D., 1866

Classical in its architectural simplicity and scale, Meigs's *Civil War Unknowns Monument* immediately gave visible form to the nation's need to honor its fallen who had no known names or graves. It was a form similar in shape to what the Quartermaster General placed over his own grave in the family plot at Arlington: a sarcophagus, sharply contrasting with the starkly realistic memorial Meigs erected over his son's grave.

Another memorial to the unknown Civil War dead, similar in design to Meigs's Arlington monument, is known as the *Tomb of the Unknown Soldier*. It was erected by the US government at the Cold Harbor National Cemetery in Mechanicsville, Virginia, in 1877.

*

Nearly fifty years later, Fabian Ware's work with the British Red Cross made him keenly aware of the alarming number of soldiers killed early in the Great War. As the war continued, the number of dead to be buried and commemorated increased to alarming proportions. Ware suggested that an organization with powers broader than those of the British Red Cross was needed. He argued successfully for the creation of a new Commission, which would go beyond the functions of registration and burial of the dead. In May 1917, the Imperial War Graves Commission (IWGC) was created, among whose charges were the commemoration of the dead, known, unknown, and missing.

Funds had already been allocated to commemorate the unknown remains of soldiers with the erection of a headstone on the grave indicating "Unknown" status. Additional monies had to be forthcoming for the proposed three large memorials to the missing commemorating the battles at Ypres, the Somme, and at Amiens. There were also smaller memorials to the missing at Armentières, Bethune, Arras, St. Quentin, Tyne Cot, Nieuport, Cambrai, La Ferté-sous-Jouarre and Soissons as well. According to the Commission, all were to be viewed as "general memorials to the war and not alone memorials to the missing."

Not all Commission members were in agreement regarding the various means of commemoration. Some Commission members were troubled by the fact that money had already been allocated to commemorate the Missing in the erection of headstones on unidentified graves. Why should more money be made available to duplicate the same information on another memorial?

There was also the issue of duplication of other battle exploit memorials, which presumably each of the Dominion governments would have the liberty to erect. These would be memorials distinct from those proposed by the IWGC. (In the end, that is what each of the Dominion governments chose to do: erect memorials to their own dead, creating a new and distinct sense of national identity apart from the British Empire.) But Kenyon argued that too many memorials of an imposing scale would "largely destroy the effect" of the large memorials proposed by Lutyens (*Memorial to the Missing of the Somme at Thiepval*) and Blomfield (*Menin Gate Memorial to the Missing at Ypres*). "It is impossible," Kenyon argued, "to commemorate in brass or stone all the memorable deeds of the war, and those [memorials] which are erected should be few and fit."

*

Although not the first to be completed, the *Menin Gate* designed by Sir Reginald Blomfield is one of the major memorials to the missing specifically honoring the British Empire forces serving in the Ypres (Belgium) sector. A professor of Architecture at the Royal Academy schools and president of the Royal Institute of British Architects, Blomfield was also an established practitioner of the classical tradition of architecture and had published *A History of Renaissance Architecture in England* in 1897. It was no surprise that he was awarded this important commission.

A major thoroughfare since the city's founding, the route of the *Menin Gate* was the principal road used by troops of the British Empire as they marched out of the city to battle. As one critic observed, "practically every division on the Western Front passed through Ypres at one time or another… its defense stands to the British Army as Verdun is to the French." The memorial would rise amidst the vast ruins of the war-torn Ypres landscape so vividly depicted in British artist Paul Nash's painting, *The Menin Road,* painted in 1919 for the British War Memorials scheme.

Blomfield's *Menin Gate* is an archi-

Sir Reginald Blomfield, *The Menin Gate Memorial to the Missing,* 1927. Ypres, Belgium.

Paul Nash, *The Menin Road,* 1919. Collection, Imperial War Museum, London. (Art IWM, No. 2242)

Blomfield, Details, *The Menin Gate.*

tectural structure whose purpose is commemorative and utilitarian. It is both a Hall of Memory commemorating nearly 55,000 missing soldiers of the British Empire and a functioning gateway/bridge connecting the newer and older Ypres. It is an extended triumphal arch through which vehicular and pedestrian traffic constantly pass. A drive-through temple, it occupies the site of the former eastern gate of the older medieval city, spanning a moat-like Ypres River—which originally defined the perimeter of the city. Contemporary postcards speak of the gate as a Valhalla, calling it a "memorial of British heroes." Viewed from the ramparts, the structure visually invokes the monumentality of a Greek temple, a triumphal Roman arch, the Roman Pantheon, and Egyptian funerary temples. In the dramatic barrel vaulted interior space known as the Hall of Memory, the coffered ceiling is lit by three bronze skylight oculi. An inscription authored by Rudyard Kipling, who was a member of the IWGC, is incised on a projected shallow tablet of the arched doorway to the exterior loggia and reads: "Here are recorded the names of officers and men who fell in Ypres Salient, but to whom the fortune of war denied the known and honoured burial given to their comrades in death." Above the inscription is carved in smaller script, "*Ad Majorem Dei Gloriam*" ("To the Greater Glory of God"). Similarly patriotic phrases such as *Pro Patria Et Pro Rege* ("For King and Country") are found on each of the entryways to the Hall of Memory.

The number of missing soldiers' names to be inscribed on the walls of the *Menin Gate* dictated the complexity of Blomfield's architectural composition. Pavilions constructed of red face brick and white mortar joints banded near the cornice in dressed Portland stone created interior spaces entered through a severe rectangular opening by means of two shallow steps from the ground plane. The interior walls also bear the names of the missing. Stretched between and bridging the two pavilions is a shallow loggia whose back wall also lists the names of the missing. In front of the wall, six severe Doric columns rhythmically support a lintel capped by the cornice of the overall gate. From the south ramparts, a more formal, temple-like effect is especially prominent.

The overall scale and visual language of commemoration expressed in the *Menin Gate* and other memorials to the missing created a compositional elegance appropriate and fitting for the task at hand. Blomfield, Lutyens, and Baker—the three principal architects of the memorials to the missing—shared a stylistic affinity described by great architectural art historian Sir Nikolaus Pevsner as "Imperial Classic"; an architectural language steeped in the classical tradition of Christopher Wren and Palladio. Popular at the turn of the nineteenth century, these sophisticated styles expressed the optimism of a yet unshaken Empire, an assertive "fashionable classicism" which both reiterated the established forms of England's glorious past and effectively transposed the sentiment and expression, the pomp and circumstance, the faith and belief in the Empire. These were echoed as well in the stately music of Edward Elgar and the measured patriotic verse of Rudyard Kipling. As ponderous as these interchangeable architectural vocabularies might seem today, at the time they were seen as appropriate solutions to commemorate the fallen soldiers of the mother country.

Not everyone was moved by the *Menin Gate* nor viewed it as a "memorial to British heroes." The respected architectural and social critic W.R. Lethaby questioned the need or the wisdom of erecting memorials to the war dead at all. In 1922, he wrote, "The best of all memorials would be those which helped speedily to organize the drifting masses of men who are returning to 'promises'… and the unproductive monuments will not do that… These designs in the 'grand manner' are pompous nullities."

Siegfried Sassoon, war poet and veteran, asked in his poem, "On Passing the New Menin Gate" from 1928:

Blomfield, Detail, *The Menin Gate*. Names of soldiers from India.

Who will remember, passing through this Gate
The unheroic Dead who fed the guns?
Who shall absolve the foulness of their fate,
Those doomed, conscripted, unvictorious ones?

For Sassoon, such grandly scaled architectural memorials were ill-conceived "pomp"—mere piles of "peace complacent stone" whose "intolerably nameless names" could not begin to "absolve the foulness of their fate."

Here was the world's worst wound. And here with pride
"Their name Liveth for evermore" The Gateway claims …
Well might the Dead who struggled in the slime
Rise and deride this sepulchre of crime.

Sassoon and other war poets spoke to the reality of the brutal suffering of the soldiers. Protracted trench warfare created unspeakable conditions. In a despairing note to his wife telling of his experiences at the front, painter Paul Nash likened the battlefields to "one huge grave … unspeakable, godless, hopeless." Nash's *Void* exhibited in 1919 was viewed as an image fulgent with "squalor" … a savage exposure of sterility." After seeing Nash's *Void* at the 1920 Toronto exhibit of the Canadian War Memorials Exhibition, Canadian artist A.Y. Jackson concluded that the small thirty-inch painting said more about war "than all of the big twenty foot canvases put together."

No visual monuments to the fallen, known, unknown, or missing—productive or unproductive—would appear to be capable of embodying commemorative meaning. But failure do so was not an option.

Thus at the July 24, 1927 unveiling and dedication of the *Menin Gate*, the *London Sunday Times* described the memorial as being "of the austere beauty which befits the grand but cruel memories which it recalls," and noted its "simple grandeur." The journalist reported that a great pilgrimage from England attended the ceremonies, where hymns were sung, prayers were offered, and many addresses were given, including by the King of Belgium. *The Literary Digest* of August 1927 noted that the unveiling service concluded with "Last Post" played by the buglers of the Second Somerset Light Infantry. The pipers of the First Battalion of the Scots Guards played a lament ("Flowers of the Forest"), which was followed by one minute of silence and the Reveille. It was a moving unveiling to be followed by similar services as other memorials to the missing were completed. Since 1928, a year after its dedication, a nightly ceremony continues to take place at the *Menin Gate*. Citizens and tourists gather at the gate at 7:45 p.m., the buglers arrive at 7:55 when traffic is stopped, and "Last Post" marking

Paul Nash, *Void,* 1918. Transfer from Canadian War Memorials, 1921. (Courtesy National Gallery of Canada, Ottawa. No.8650)

Sir Edwin Lutyens, *Thiepval Memorial to the Missing of the Somme,* 1932. France.

the end of the day is played at 8:00 p.m. It is a powerful nightly ritual, reminiscent in its simplicity and mournful overtones of the last line of Wilfred Owen's poem, "Anthem for Doomed Youth": "And each slow dusk a drawing down of blinds."

*

Of the other major memorials to the missing, *Thiepval* continues to draw attention from both critics and admirers for its scale and placement. Designed by Sir Edwin Lutyens, it is the corresponding Memorial to the Missing of the Somme in France to Blomfield's Memorial to the Missing in Ypres, Belgium. Lutyens' overscaled Arch commemorates both soldiers of the British Empire and of France who came to the relief of those fighting the Germans and who died in the Somme offensive—a disastrous debacle, which historian Liddell Hart described as "both the glory and the graveyard of Kitch-

Ivan Mestrovic, Detail, *Canadian Phalanx,* 1919. Veterans
Administration Buildings, Wellington Street, Ottawa.

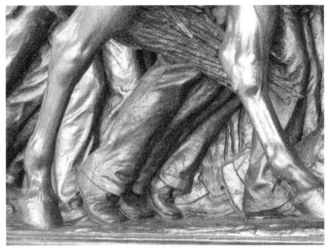

Augustus Saint-Gaudens, Detail, *Robert Gould Shaw Memorial,* 1884.
Boston Common, Boston, Massachusetts.

Henry Schrady, Detail, *Ulysses S. Grant Memorial,* 1902-1924. Washington, DC

ener's Army." The July 1,1916 attack of the Germans, he notes,

> Marked the heaviest British loss of any day's fighting in the war [largely due to the] revival of formations that were akin to the eighteenth-century in their formalism and lack of manoeuvering power. Men … almost shoulder to shoulder, in a symmetrical well-dressed alignment [were] taught to advance steadily upright at a slow walk with their rifles held aslant in front of them, bayonets upwards, so as to catch the eye of the observant enemy … infantry automata.

The image of soldiers as mechanized automata marching shoulder to shoulder was both brutal and convincing as rendered in sharply chiseled stone by Croatian sculptor Ivan Mestrovic, whose relief sculpture entitled *Canadian Phalanx*, commissioned by the Canadian War Memorials, is now placed in Ottawa between the Veterans Administration Buildings. These and other renderings of soldiers in World War I contrast dramatically with the more pathetic and specific renderings of individual American soldiers marching to battle as seen in Saint-Gaudens' *Robert Gould Shaw Memorial* or Schrady's *Memorial to Ulysses S. Grant*—both more organically rendered in clay and cast in bronze.

By mid-November 1916, the Battle of the Somme was over and British Empire Forces had lost some 125,000 soldiers. Those who could be identified were buried in the adjoining cemetery over which the *Thiepval* arch looms, still strangely out of scale in its rural agricultural landscape. Sited on a high plateau, the memorial is of such magnitude as to be visible from a great distance and is constructed of dark-red brick and dressed white stone. Lutyens composed a block-like, stepped form of interlocking triumphal arches. A central barrel vaulted, coffered arch springs from two large piers, which in turn are pierced by arches supported by two additional stepped-back forms also pierced by arches. The four supporting blocks—two on each side of the central arched form—are faced in white stone, both on the exterior and in the interior galleries, onto which are inscribed the names of the missing. The result is a continuous white wall, which makes the heaviness of the overall massive form visually lighter. The eighty foot high central arch terminates in a crenellated tower, on which are mounted two flagstaffs—one flying the French Tricolor, the other the British Union Jack. Overall, the structure is one hundred fifty feet in height and sits on a low podium edged in white above the brick base. Stairs lead to Lutyens's Great Stone, dramatically placed under the central vaulted arch and functioning as a masonry canopy—baldacchino-like—that shields the altar from the elements.

The site is a gradually sloped landscape with gravel walkways directing the visitor down to a small military cemetery with graves of unknown French and British soldiers. Small crosses for the French, standard gravestones for the British. The graves flank either side of Blomfield's Cross of Sacrifice. They create the rear boundary of the small cemetery and provide a focal point out and below the Memorial Arch directly in line with the Great Stone. Inscribed on the Cross are words

Sir Edwin Lutyens, Detail, *Thiepval Memorial to the Missing*. France.

Sir Herbert Baker, *Tyne Cot Memorial to the Missing*, 1927. Belgium.

that summarize the terrible toll of the First World War: "That the world may remember the common sacrifice of two and a half million dead. Here have been laid side by side soldiers of France and of the British Empire in eternal comradeship."

The sources and precedents for the *Thiepval Memorial* are complex. Architectural historian Vince Scully saw a "touching relationship" between *Thiepval* and the local "neo-Greco pilgrimage church" of Notre Dame de Brebières in Albert, a church troops marched past upon arrival. A more obvious source is Lutyens's 1917 *All India Memorial Arch of 1917*, a 139-foot triumphal arch anchoring King's Way in New Delhi with the Viceroy's House, a focusing device similar to Chalgrin's placement of the Arc de Triomph in Paris on the Champs-Élysées in alignment with the Palace of the Louvre. Neither of those precedents explains, however, the emotionally jarring experience of seeing a monumental urban form in a rural landscape—an experience emotionally described by Scully when he first visited and detailed the monument at Thiepval as one that "menaces the living [and] ferociously guards the dead." He continued:

> The monument looms over us, stepping mountainously up and back …
> like one of the American skyscrapers of the 1920s. It is also an enormous monster, its tondi are eyes, its high arch
> screams. It is the open mouth of death … Absolute pain and nothingness.

Christopher Hussey, a Lutyens biographer, saw *Thiepval* in a less menacing light. "There is sublimity in this great abstraction of pure architecture," he noted. "To the emotional mind, its multitude of arches may represent portals to the four quarters of the wide horizon, ever open for the spirits of the lost."[21]

*

Thiepval and *Menin Gate* are the two major British Empire Forces memorials to the missing in Europe. The National Battlefields Memorial (Midleton) Committee, however, reached the conclusion after much debate that additional memorials should be erected.

Thus, Sir Herbert Baker was given the commission to design the *Tyne Cot Memorial* at Tyne Cot Cemetery in Belgium. It was to commemorate 35,000 officers and men whose graves were unknown. Incorporating three German pillboxes within the cemetery grounds (the largest Commonwealth War Graves cemetery of World War I), the fourth pillbox forms the foundation for Blomfield's Cross of Sacrifice. Baker defined the perimeter of the cemetery with vertical panels inscribed with the names of the missing listed by rank and regiment. Other memorials were built as well, including by each of the Dominions to memorialize their fallen and missing.

The Canadian government, through the agency of the Canadian Battlefields Commission, at first considered "Hill 62" in France to be the site for a Canadian national memorial. But after further consideration, Vimy was chosen as the place to commemorate Canada's fallen and missing dead. Vimy ridge was chosen to be both a national memorial to all Canadians who fought in the Great War as well as a memorial to the missing and unknown Canadian dead in France. The names of the unknown and missing Canadian soldiers who died in Belgium were to be inscribed on the *Menin Gate* monument in Ypres.

Sculptor W.S. Allward's monument design was accepted by the Commission and erected at Vimy. It stands over two hundred feet wide overall with two twin pylons that rise to a height of 120 feet. Altogether, some twenty carved figures in an around the memorial create an elaborate iconography which include allegorical representations of Justice, Charity,

---

21   Christopher Hussey, "The Life of Sir Edwin Lutyens," London: Country Life, 1953. p.475.

W.S. Allward, *Canadian National Vimy Memorial*, 1936. France.

Peace, Sacrifice, Guardian Angels, a Dying Soldier, and a representation of Canada. One wall is engraved with the names in alphabetical order of the 11,285 missing Canadian soldiers who died in France. Also engraved on the elaborate monument to Canada's missing in France are the words: "To the valour of their countrymen in the Great War and in memory of the 60,000 dead this monument is raised by the people of Canada."

More sculptural than architectural, overtly theatrical and stage-like in its composition, the scale of Allward's *National Memorial at Vimy* rivals that of Lutyens's *Thiepval*, but addresses no historical or stylistic precedent by which to judge its success. By present standards, its narrative, figurative content seems anomalous. Yet at the time of its dedication on July 26, 1936, it was embraced as an overwhelming success. Great Britain's King Edward VIII—one of several presenters at the opening ceremony—declared, "We raise this memorial to Canadian warriors. It is an inspired expression in stone... Canada's salute to her fallen sons." The *National Memorial at Vimy* changed the country's perceptions of itself as well as the perceptions of the rest of the world after 1918. Lieutenant Colonel D.E. Mcintyre, writing in 1967 on the centennial of Canada's founding, noted that:

> By this victory at Vimy Canada achieved at one bound what years of political and commercial effort had not accomplished. Prior to 1914 Canada was a Dominion of about eight million people ... She was looked upon by most outsiders(quite mistakenly) as a British colony and a pleasant place to spend a vacation hunting and fishing ... After her baptismal blood bath [the Great War] however, she grew up and achieved nationhood.

W.S. Allward, Detail, *Canadian National Vimy Memorial.*

W.S. Allward, Detail, *Canadian National Vimy Memorial.*

The United States, although joining the Allies later in World War I (April 6,1917) also commemorated its missing and unknown dead in Flanders and in France. Some fifteen monuments and memorials were erected. Commemoration of the fallen was principally in the form of inscriptions in local cemetery chapels.

Within a decade of War's end, the most accessible and successful public monuments erected to commemorate the dead were neither on nor near the battlefields where they had fought. Public and very visible forms of commemoration were erected instead in London, Ottawa, and Washington, DC. Lutyens's *Cenotaph* in Whitehall, London; The *National War Monument* and the

    Memorial Chamber in the newly rebuilt *"Peace Tower"* for the Houses of Parliament in Ottawa; and the *Tomb of the Unknown Soldier* in Arlington National Cemetery are commemorative memorials placed in national capitals visited today by millions.

Cram and Ferguson. Detail, *Names of the Missing*, 1937. Chapel Interior, Aisne-Marne American Cemetery, Belleau, France.

CHAPTER FOUR

Hidden in Plain Sight: Public Monuments and Private Memorials

"The stone statues of the abstract Union Soldier grow slimmer and younger each year—wasp-waisted, they doze over muskets and muse through their sideburns."
—Robert Lowell, "For the Union Dead"

ON OCTOBER 30, 1863, the State Legislature of Vermont passed the following Resolution: "Any town may instruct its selectmen to erect a monument or monuments to the memory of citizens of such town, dying in the service of the country, during the present war, and may appropriate a sum of money sufficient to defray the expense of such erection." Less than three years later, the Vermont town of St. Johnsbury voted to raise $10,000 to erect a monument to commemorate the town's sons killed in the Civil War. Half the money would come from the town and the other half would be donations from private individuals. With $5,000, the Soldiers' Monument Committee (led by local industrialist and future Governor Horace Fairbanks) hired Vermont native Larkin G. Mead, Jr. to create a suitable marble statue at the artist's studio in Florence, Italy. In 1858, Mead had sculpted the allegorical figure of Ceres for the dome of the state capitol in Montpelier, so he was a logical choice. He was later given the prestigious commission to work on the tomb of President Lincoln in Springfield, Illinois.

In the summer of 1868, the statue *America* reached New York City and was transported north to St. Johnsbury. The granite foundation and pedestal were in place. It was inaugurated with imposing ceremonies on August 20. A procession through the town's streets included Gilmore's brass band of Boston, various Masonic organizations, and a wagon containing thirty-six little girls dressed in white and representing the different states of the now restored Union. Other vehicles carried a young lady representing Peace, officers, and orators of the day: disabled soldiers and friends of deceased soldiers. Veterans, fire companies, and citizens marched through several streets of the village to the Court House grounds. After suitable oratory, the monument was unveiled to a tumult of cheering. *America* was a draped female figure eight feet tall, holding a wreath of oak and laurel in her left hand, while her right rested on a sword. Her sash was studded with stars, her girdle decorated with shields and on her brow rested a diadem of thirteen stars. At her feet, an eagle perched with its talons on a copy of the Constitution. The inscription on the base read, "In Honor of the St. Johnsbury Volunteers Who Sacrificed Their Lives in Defence of the Union." Around the base were inscribed the names of eighty St. Johnsbury soldiers who died, the causes of their death, and the battles where they fought. Mead, the sculptor, was introduced to the assembly. Governor Paul Dillingham spoke. Prayer was offered by Reverend John H. Woodward, chaplain of the First Vermont Cavalry. On either side of the memorial were placed two twenty-pound Naval Parrot cannons obtained from the war department. Every half an hour, cannon shots were fired from "an eminence some little distance in a north-easterly direction."

In the years that followed, dozens of Vermont towns followed St. Johnsbury in honoring their war dead. Immediately after the War, the monuments tended to be symbolic, allegorical, and unique. But twenty to thirty years later, as veterans were dying at an increasing rate, the monuments took on a martial tone and form—generally the standing sentinel model. Finding such figures was easier, because by then a number of companies were manufacturing these statues by the hundreds in a variety of designs. The industrialization that had facilitated more deaths on the battlefield also made easier the memorialization of those dead.

In honoring the dead of the American Civil War and World War I, the survivors shared a common philosophy. The dead were to be publicly commemorated with monuments for both the common soldier and the ranked officer. Both wars had reaped devastating losses. In some instances, ten to twenty percent of the male population of a community never returned home. Growing public sentiment concurred that the grief felt for the dead was not just a family matter, but a bereavement experienced and to be shared collectively by the larger community—a civic responsibility as well as a moral obligation to honor and commemorate their fallen.

Today, many of these monuments have been neglected and forgotten. Not intentionally, of course, but their familiarity has made them almost invisible; they are hidden in plain sight. Some have been camouflaged by new trees and foliage or replaced in public view by swing sets, new statues, or public art. In this chapter, we will seek to retrieve these statues from the mists of time and contemptuous familiarity, from vandalism and obscurity, and weave them back into the public space and the public eye. We want to recapture moments when no one doubted the duty to mourn publicly.

Our analytical morphology for this study has four components that often overlap. The first slice of analysis is the subject/object. Is it an allegorical figure, an anonymous soldier, a known general, a gun, an obelisk, a stone cairn? The second is the location of the statues, such as a public space, a battlefield, a cemetery, or an employer property. The third angle is the source. Who gave the statue: a town, a regiment, a private individual, an employer? What were the circumstances? Finally, we discuss the configuration of the monument. Is it three dimensions, a bas-relief? Is it a single figure or a group? What of the scale of the monument in relation to its final location? All the monuments we will examine were meant to assuage grief and arouse a sense of triumph—to speak of sacrifice but not despair, of purpose but not futility. Just as the monuments would long outlive flesh and blood, they would convey eternal gratitude and honor. The creed of all was the

Larkin Mead, *America*, 1868. St. Johnsbury, Vermont.

Randolph Rogers, *Soldiers National Monument*, 1866-69. Gettysburg, Pennsylvania.

Carl Conrads, *The Private Soldier Monument, "Old Simon,"* 1876. Antietam, Maryland.

"sanguinary imperative" which promises that these honored soldiers did not die in vain.

*

The commemoration of two of the Civil War's most decisive battles, Antietam and Gettysburg, began within five years of the war's end. The Soldier's National Monument (1866-'69) at Gettysburg is a multi-figured work whose crowning figure is an allegorical representation of Liberty. She is placed atop a column sixty feet high and the base is surrounded by seated figures (two female, two male) representing History, War, Peace, and Plenty. The marble sculptures by Randolph Rogers led to further Civil War memorial commissions for the sculptor. Inscribed on the monument is part of Lincoln's Gettysburg address. Sometimes referred to as "the national monument to sorrow," the memorial was funded by subscription of states whose soldiers died in the Battle of Gettysburg.

By contrast, the realistic rendering and best-known representation of the common soldier of the Civil War was dedicated at Antietam National Cemetery in 1880. The cornerstone for the monument was laid in September 1867. Designed by sculptor Carl Conrads, with a pedestal designed by George Keller, the monument known variously as *The Private Soldier Monument, The American Volunteer,* and *Old Simon* was exhibited at the 1876 Columbian Centennial Exposition in Philadelphia, where it was seen by millions of visitors. The grey granite figure stands slightly over twenty-one feet high atop a pedestal of similar dimensions resulting in a colossal monument over forty feet in height. On the face of the pedestal are carved the words, "Not For Themselves But For Their Country." Below the inscription and in low relief are carved flags and emblems of battle with the date "September 17, 1862."

The final placement of the statue at Antietam is at the center of the cemetery where remains of nearly five thousand Union soldiers from the Battles of Antietam, South Mountain, and other actions in Maryland are buried, their graves arranged by state in a semi-circle around the base. The significant placement and immense scale of *Old Simon,* plus the stately pose and expressive features of his face, impart a religious overtone to the work. Sadness, mourning, and sacrifice are the predominant emotions expressed by the monument. Like French's Concord *Minuteman,* Conrads' *American Soldier* at Antietam became the iconic image of war's sacrifice and commemoration, a model for many civic monuments erected throughout America after the Civil War.

Variations on a Theme

In some monuments with a single figure, the sculptural composition is a tiered format with representative branches of military service or allegorical representations of Liberty (Columbia), Victory, or Peace. There are slight variations of the treatment of the central figure, which include a flag-bearer or an older bearded veteran with bowed head. Other civic monuments feature a solitary soldier with idiosyncratic characteristics such as the one depicted in the monument in front of the library in Wilmington, Vermont. It shows a soldier whose proportions and facial treatment—deep-set eyes—are markedly distinct from the prototype.

Variations from the paradigm appear with greater frequency in monuments south of the Mason-Dixon line. *Appomattox,* a lone soldier with downcast head and hat removed, no weapon at his side, was erected by local citizens in Alexandria, Virginia, in 1889, and was prominently placed in the center of Washington Street.

The Confederate monument in Waycross, Georgia, sited across from the central Railroad Station and hotel, depicts a single soldier/farmer, broad hat askew, rifle resting on his right shoulder atop a granite column, the base inscribed with a dedication to the Confederate dead and the lines, "Eternal Right Though All Things Fail Can Never Be Made Wrong. Many Of Whom Gave All, And All Of Whom Gave Much."

Left, Marshall and Seward Jones, *Middlebury to her Soldiers*, 1904-1905. Middlebury, Vermont.

Above, Anonymous, *Civil War Soldier,"In Memory of our Country's Defenders,"* c.1905. Wilmington, Vermont.

Right, John Adams Elder and M. Caspar Buber,*"Appomattox,"*1889. Alexandria, Virginia. (Courtesy of Wikimedia Commons)

The Ladies Memorial Association of Union Springs, Alabama, raised a monument to the Confederate dead that was dedicated on March 29,1895. Inscribed on the base supporting a standing soldier at "parade rest" dressed in common clothes, hat tilted back on his head, both hands gripping the gun's barrel, are the lines, "Died on the field of battle, 'twas noble thus to die. God smiles on valiant soldiers. Their record is on high." Originally placed in the center of the main street in front of the Bullock County Court House, the monument was later removed to a cemetery in back of the library overlooking graves of unknown Confederate dead.

Far left, Anonymous, *Confederate Soldiers Memorial*, 1893. Union Springs, Alabama.

Left, Daniel J. Perry, *Goddess of Liberty*, 1868. Swanton, Vermont.

Above, Anonymous, Stannard Womens Relief Corps, *Civil War Monument*, 1907. City Hall Park, Burlington, Vermont.

There are civic monuments whose principal image and theme—like *America* in St. Johnsbury, Vermont—are allegorical or mythological. *The Goddess of Liberty* by local artist Daniel Perry erected in Swanton, Vermont, in 1868 shows a Grecian maiden with classical drapery falling from her shoulders, holding an upright standing flag at her left side. She is closer in conception to French painter Eugene Delacroix's *Liberty Leading the People* [1830] than to Mead's sculpture of *America*. Sculpted in marble from quarries in Rutland and Isle La Motte, *Goddess* is placed in the town park, her base bearing the names of the twenty-eight soldiers from Swanton who died in the Civil War.

Great Barrington, Massachusetts, can boast of one of the most elegant Civil War monuments: the eight-foot high bronze *Victory,* dated 1876. It was placed in front of the newly built Georgian-style town hall. *Victory,* with both wings outspread, stands on a globe of gold, both arms stretched, the left hand bearing a laurel wreath, the right hand an olive branch.[22] Inspired by a fresco fragment from Pompeii, the three-dimensional rendering by sculptor Truman Howe Bartlett was the idea of John H. Coffing, a member of the monument committee and principal contributor to the project. Civil war monuments whose forms were more abstract and non-figurative were less common. Cannon, obelisks and geometric shapes adorned with emblems of the various armed forces can be found both in public spaces and in private cemeteries.

MEMORIALS AND MONUMENTS TO INDIVIDUALS

While the majority of civic monuments are to the citizens of the community who served and died—common soldiers and officers alike—there were often monuments to individual Civil War officers, paid for by civic groups, wealthy individuals, fellow veterans, or families of the fallen. In Burlington, Vermont, two of the most famous veterans to return from the war were honored with life size statues: Brevet Major General William Wells and Major General George J. Stannard.

The Wells statue is an animated rendering of the general in full military dress with sword in hand and spurs on striding boots by sculptor Otto Schweizer. It is prominently displayed in Burlington's Battery Park, a historic urban green dedicated to the War of 1812 which overlooks Lake Champlain. Wells's statue is a replica of the original one first placed at Gettysburg in 1914. Beneath the striding statue of Wells is a bas-relief bronze tablet depicting the Vermont First Calvary charge against Law's Alabama Brigade. It was dedicated at Gettysburg fifty years after the Battle of July 3, 1863.

A life-sized one-armed sleeveless statue of General George Jerrison Stannard by sculptor Karl Gerhardt marks the general's grave in Burlington's Lakeview Cemetery. A bronze tablet at the base of the statue narrates Stannard's exploits and ends with the phrase, "Sleep, Soldier, Sleep. Thy Battles all are O'er." Attesting to his vital role during Pickett's charge, an earlier bronze statue (1889) of the general in full military dress is atop the State of Vermont monument at Gettysburg—a sixty foot Corinthian column of granite with the Seal of the State of Vermont at its base.

Military units, all state-based, rushed to populate revered battle sites with monuments to their hallowed dead. At Antietam, survivors erected six inverted cannon to commemorate the six generals—three Union, three Confederate—who were killed on a single day. At Gettysburg, close to 1300 state, individual, and unit memorials considerably varied in their form and style appeared in the next four decades. Far from the battlefields, regiments put up memorials to their own who died in battle. John Quincy Adams Ward was commissioned by the New York Seventh Regiment to create a monument to the fifty-eight members of the regiment who died in the Civil War. Erected in 1869, the single Union soldier resting on his gun stands on a large granite pedestal with rondels designed by architect Richard Morris Hunt. Sculptor and architect

---

22   The rendering of the allegorical figure is stylistically close and may even have been the source for Saint-Gaudens' treatment of the "Angel of Peace" from the monument to *General Tecumseh Sherman,* 1903.

53

J.Otto Schweitzer, *General William Wells Monument,* 1913-14. Gettysburg, Pennsylvania and Battery Park, Burlington, Vermont.

Karl Gerhardt, *Brigadier General George Stannard,* 1889. Lakeview Cemetery, Burlington, Vermont.

would collaborate again on the 1883 Lafayette statue for the University of Vermont.

Civil War monuments honoring specific individuals—generals, political leaders, and heroes—thus began to appear. Some were publicly funded, others paid for by private donors. The equestrian image of a leader astride his horse remained a favored form of commemoration whether sculpted in the round or rendered in high or low relief. Equestrian monuments have a long history in Western culture. The equestrian portrait of Roman emperor Marcus Aurelius, erected in 175 CE for the Forum in Rome, embodied in its pose and countenance qualities of strength, victory, even god-like status. Military and political leaders including Charlemagne, Napoleon, and Field Marshal Earl Haig have been portrayed mounted

William Rudolf and John Duncan, *Monument to the Irish Brigade*, 1888. Gettysburg, Pennsylvania.

Anonymous, *Mortuary Cannon memorial to Union Maj. General Israel Richardson*, 1898. Antietam, Maryland. (Photo by Peter Fischer)

Anonymous, *Drum Monument to the 51st Pennsylvania Volunteers Regiment*. Antietam, Maryland.

on a horse. The form elevates them above the common foot soldier to emphasize both their abilities and their status as heads of armies or of state.

*

"And this, fellow citizens, is why, after the great generals have had their monuments, and long after the abstract soldier's monuments have been reared on every village green, we have chosen to take Robert Shaw and his regiment as the first soldier's monument to be raised to a particular set of comparatively undistinguished men."
—William James, dedication speech upon the unveiling of the Shaw Monument, May 31, 1897

Above, Augustus Saint-Gaudens, *Memorial to Robert Gould Shaw and the Massachusetts Fifty-Fourth Regiment*, 1884-1897. Boston Common, Boston, Massachusetts.

Left, John Quincy Adams Ward, *Seventh New York Regiment Memorial*, 1869. New York City.

The equestrian monument in bronze by Augustus Saint-Gaudens depicting Robert Gould Shaw and the black soldiers of the 54th Massachusetts Volunteer Regiment under his command is one of America's greatest public monuments. The idea of creating a memorial to Shaw was originally promoted by former-slave J.D. Smith whose commitment to the proposal was endorsed by the Shaw family for whom he had worked. As funds multiplied, the city of Boston became committed to the project with the proviso that the finished work would be prominently placed on the Boston Common across from the Massachusetts Statehouse. Executed in both high and low relief, the life size narrative tableau cast in bronze depicts an allegorical figure of the Angel of Peace in low relief with olive branch extended, leading Shaw on horseback with his black soldiers on foot as they marched down Beacon Street in Boston in May of 1863. The monument commemorates the death of Shaw and at least half of his troops in the attack on Fort Wagner, South Carolina, two months later.

Shaw sits erect on his horse looking dead ahead as do his troops who march with long, forceful strides beside and in back of him, their forward movement from left to right across the composition mirroring that of the steed. Shaw's right arm holds a sword, his left hand pulls the reins taut, bringing the head and neck of the horse back to a posture of resolve and tension echoing his own. The guns and blanket-rolls of the soldiers—two and three deep—are remarkably life-like in their depiction. Shaw modeled the faces of the troops from numerous individuals who came to his studio. The flags extend upward toward the representation of the allegorical Angel of Peace.

Set within an architectural surround originally designed by H.H. Richardson and completed by architect Stanford White, the monument is placed slightly above the ground plane parallel with the sidewalk. Its placement effectively engages the viewer, allowing one to examine the detailed treatment of the soldiers and of Shaw. As a result, viewers are invited to become a part of the ensemble.[23]

Saint-Gaudens' last realized work was the life-size equestrian monument to Union Army General William Tecumseh Sherman. At the time of Sherman's death in 1891, the New York City Chamber of Commerce commissioned Saint-Gaudens to create the monument to be placed in a prominent public space. The sculptor's dramatic rendering of the bareheaded Sherman shows him on his horse wearing a flowing cape. Horse and rider are led by a winged Victory with olive branch outstretched. Victory steps forward and downward on a slightly raised plinth. The grey granite pedestal designed by Charles McKim is tomblike in shape, decorated with three ornamental wreaths on each side. The contrast between the sculpture and the pedestal is heightened by Saint-Gaudens' decision to gild the bronze. The golden hue to the work infers, it would seem, the apotheosis of Sherman in afterlife. Originally, Saint-Gaudens intended the work to be placed in front of the elaborate and recently completed *Grant Tomb/Mausoleum* in Riverside Park in Morningside Heights. The Grant family and Chamber of Commerce determined instead to place the work in the Grand Army Plaza, where it was dedicated in 1903.

In the South, Commander of the Confederate Northern Army of Virginia, General Robert E. Lee, was honored by his friends and compatriots with an equestrian statue in Richmond, Virginia—the former capitol of the Confederacy. Unveiled in 1890, the monument was funded by popular subscription. The statue was executed in Paris by French academic artist Jean Mercie, a professor of Drawing and Sculpture at the Ècole des Beaux Arts in Paris. The twenty-one foot high bronze statue of the bareheaded general on his horse sits atop a granite pedestal forty feet high designed by French architect Paul Pujot. The Lee statue was the first of several equestrian monuments to heroes of the Confederacy placed on Monument Avenue including Stonewall Jackson by William E. Sievers, dedicated in 1919, and a lively rendering of J.E.B. Stuart by Fred Moynihan in 1907.

The Soldiers and Sailors Arch (1889-92) in Brooklyn, New York, fuses both sculpture and architecture into a grand civic monument dedicated "To the Defenders of the Union-1861-1865." It was funded by the citizens of Brooklyn. The

---

23   The work is a visually accessible because it is roughly at eye level, which is not the case with the 126-foot high *Soldiers and Sailors Monument* dedicated in 1877. Erected a short distance away on the Boston Common, the eleven-foot high allegorical representation of America standing on an extended "Victory" column is beyond one's visual field of direct engagement.

Far left, Augustus Saint-Gaudens, *William Tecumseh Sherman Monument*, 1892-1903. Grand Army Plaza, Brooklyn, New York.

Left, Jean Mercie, *General Robert E. Lee Monument*, 1890. Richmond, Virginia. (Photograph courtesy of Wikimedia Commons)

eighty foot high triumphal arch is the focal point of Grand Army Plaza, the gateway to Prospect Park. General William Tecumseh Sherman spoke at the laying of the cornerstone for the monument in 1889. The monument is a collaboration of many architects, landscape architects (John Duncan, Stanford White, Frederick Law Olmstead, and Calvert Vaux), and sculptors (Frederick Macmonies, William Rudolf O'Donovan, and Thomas Eakins). John Duncan, the principal designer of the triumphal arch, effectively quotes historic architectural forms—Arc de Triomphe, Arch of Titus—as he also did when referencing the Mausoleum of Halicarnassus as the prototype for his design of *Grant's Tomb* (1891-1897) in New York City. The elaborate sculptural elements on the exterior of the Arch—the Victory Quadriga, allegorical representations of the Army and Navy—overshadow the more personal and particular renderings of President Lincoln and General Grant who are depicted on horseback on the interior opening of the arch. Grant sits erect in his saddle, looking straight ahead; Lincoln looks to his right at Grant, his hat in hand in a gesture of acknowledgement and gratitude.

World War I
British Tommies and Empire Soldiers

At a civic level, public monuments and memorials to World War I dead became as pervasive in town centers throughout the British Empire as the Civil War monuments were in the United States. Also similarly, a single soldier representing both officers and men was a common civic monument to those who served and died in battle. But there was also considerable variety in the architectural forms and the sources of patronage. Many monuments were raised not just by civic organizations, but by employers, regiments, and national organizations as well.

Many of the Great War monuments in North America included stones from the various battlefields abroad on which the soldiers fought and died. In front of the granite *First World War Memorial* in Phillipsburg, Quebec, stones from major battlefields in which Canadians fought are arranged in a circular pattern on the ground. The front of the granite monument is inscribed with lines from the popular British poem by Sir Henry Newbolt entitled *"Vitaï Lampada"* ("Pass on the Torch of Life"): "Play up! Play up! And Play the Game!" This inscription expresses the quintessential British values of chivalry and sportsmanship. These virtues—or vices, depending upon one's point of view—are implicit as well in Canadian-born John McCrae's well known poem "In Flanders Fields": "Take up our quarrel with the foe: to you with failing hands we throw the torch. Be yours to hold it high."

Similarly to the American Civil War, much of the survivors' grief from the Great War came from not being able to repatriate and bury their dead. The physical and psychic distance of the survivors from those killed overseas was expressed in a poem by Nobel Prize author and British Poet Laureate Rudyard Kipling. Lines from the poem are carved on the granite and bronze *First World War Memorial* in Sault Ste. Marie, Ontario: "From little towns in a far land we came/To save our honour and a world aflame. By little towns in a far land we sleep/And trust those things we won to you to keep."

Some monuments, such as the *First World War Memorial* in Renfrew, Ontario, included lines of bittersweet consolation such as those authored by British poet Laurence Binyon and placed under the inscription TO ALL OUR HONOURED DEAD: "They shall not grow old as we who are left grow old. Age shall not weary them nor the years condemn. At the going down of the sun and in the morning we shall remember them."

A closely related sentiment to "Play up the Game" is expressed in the inscription on the *First World War Monument* in Mattawa, Ontario. The soldier sentinel placed in a small downtown park overlooks the junction of the Ottawa and Mattawa Rivers, the historic route taken by the early *coureur des bois* who traveled inland to and from the Great Lakes. A life-size granite helmeted soldier in uniform stands at "parade rest" atop a low granite pedestal. The front of the monument depicts a relief carving of a laurel wreath within which are inscribed the dates 1914-1918. Beneath the wreath are incised the words "To perpetuate the names of our honoured dead and those who carried on in the Great War from the town of Mattawa and district. Erected by the Women's Institute." Inscribed around the base of the monument area are the names of

John Duncan and Stanford White, *Soldiers' and Sailors' Arch*, 1889-1892. Grand Army Plaza, Brooklyn, New York.

the principal battles in which the Canadians fought: Somme, Vimy Ridge, Courcelette.

Larger cities in Canada erected more elaborate and varied memorials. In the Westmount suburb of Montreal, George William Hill—one of Canada's most prolific sculptors of commemorative monuments—created a moving memorial in 1921-1922 to those who died in the Great War. Prominently placed on Sherbrooke Ave. and close to the City Hall, two bronze life-size figures are placed atop a vertical granite pedestal. A striding uniformed soldier is guided by an allegorical female figure with wings, her right arm upraised and placed slightly above the soldier. One side of the pedestal is inscribed with "Their name liveth for evermore." Low walls with architectural decoration contain and define the commemorative space and bear the names of those who died in World War I; those killed in World War II were added at a later date. The front of the monument bears the inscription, "To the men of Westmount who gave their lives in the Great War MCMXIV-MCMXVIII and in the World War MCMXXXIX-MCMXLV." One

Detail, *"Play Up, Play Up the Game."* Phillipsburg, Quebec.

side of the heightened vertical pedestal depicts, in a marble inset, a standing woman in high relief holding a stocking in her hands. There is a ball of yarn at her feet and a dog looking up at her. Both figures intimate fidelity. In the background are two images of the Canadian maple leaf and a chair over which a uniform has been draped; both are carved in shallow relief. The marble inset on the opposite depicts a nurse who looks back over her shoulder, her right hand resting on a wheelchair with an injured soldier. In both material and narrative content, the reliefs speak of activities of the living—this is in contrast with the bronze grouping above.[24]

THE YANKS: THE AMERICAN DOUGHBOY

The most ubiquitous statue from the American World War I experience was the "doughboy." Specifically, it was the *Spirit of the American Doughboy* by the Georgia sculptor E. M. Viquesney (1876-1946). Unlike standing sentinels, guarding the landscape quietly against a resurgent insurgency from the South, Viquesney's *Doughboy* and others bestirred the village green like a colossal. It charges across a no-man's land of stump, hand grenade high in the right hand, a Springfield rifle with bayonet fixed, a cry or snarl in his mouth. As many as 300 of the pressed copper statues were

Anonymous, *First World War Memorial*, n.d. Phillipsburg, Quebec.

---

24   Hill's first use the allegorical winged figure is his 1913-1919 *Monument to Georges-Étienne Cartier* in Mount Royal Park, Montréal. His most significant related war monuments can be found in Montréal West [1921]; in Ottawa, Ontario in The House of Commons [*The Nurse's Memorial*, 1924]; Charlottetown, P.E.I. [1925], and in Sherbrooke, Quebec [1926].

Coeur de Lion McCarthy, *Angel of Victory*,1921. Windsor Station, Montreal.

Anonymous, *First World War Memorial*, n.d. Mattawa, Ontario.

George William Hill, *First World War Memorial*, 1921-1922. Westmount, Montreal.

made. Viquesney didn't stop with public monuments. The iconic image was popular enough that he sold thousands of statuettes and lamps in the same theme. World War II brought that production to a close. There were other styles of doughboys, such as the one in St. Albans, Vermont, but Viquesney's was by far the most common.

MONUMENTS BY EMPLOYERS

As the war progressed, able-bodied employed men and women stepped forward, left their jobs, and served in the armed forces. By war's end, many had perished. Some of the larger employers honored their former employees with tablets, plaques, or simple monuments, almost always listing their names—the simplest act of recognition and commemoration. Closely related to the Westmount memorial and a possible source for Hill's grouping of the figures is Couer de Lion McCarthy's 1921 *Angel of Victory Monument*—the World War I memorial commissioned by the Canadian Pacific Railroad and placed in Windsor Station, Montreal. With her right arm, the Angel of Victory encircles the body of the dying soldier, lifting him upwards. Her upraised left arm holds a laurel wreath. The plaque beneath the sculpture reads:

"To commemorate those in the service of the Canadian Pacific Railway Company who, at the call of King and Country, left all that was dear to them, endured hardship, faced danger and finally passed out of sight of men by the path of duty and self sacrifice giving up their own lives that others might live in freedom. Let those who come after see to it that their names be not forgotten."

Similar statues to *The Angel of Victory* were placed in Winnipeg, Manitoba, and Vancouver, British Columbia, by the Canadian Pacific Railway Company in memory of their employees who had served in the Great War. Eaton's department stores in Montreal, Toronto, and across Canada also honored their employees with memorial plaques.

*

In Great Britain, companies and public institutions also erected monuments to honor employees who were killed in the Great War. The Victoria and Albert Museum in London honored former members of their staff with a simple tablet in Hoptonwood stone in 1920. Just inside the main entrance to the museum, renowned calligrapher and sculptor Eric Gill and his assistant, Joseph Cribb, created a wall tablet whose lunette depicts a laurel leaf in low relief. Inscribed below in simple, clear lettering, are the words, "VICTORIA AND ALBERT MUSEUM IN HONOUR OF THOSE WHO GAVE THEIR LIFE FOR THEIR COUNTRY SERVING THE KING BY LAND AND SEA IN THE GREAT WAR MCMXIV-MCMXVIII" followed by the names of sixteen staff members who died. Crimson and black ink are used in the words, which gives a heightened legibility to the memorial. Beneath the commemorative inscription and the list of names and in smaller font are the words, "Set up by subscription of the whole staff in memory of their comrades." The sup-

Top left, E.M. Viquesney, *The Spirit of the American Doughboy*, 1923. St. Albans, Vermont.

Above, J. Lyons and Co., *Memorial Obelisk*, 1922. Hammersmith, London. (Photo by William Spooner)

Bottom left, Detail, *Lyons Memorial*, 1922. (Photo by William Spooner)

porting brackets for the tablet are initialed by the two artists.

At the end of the war, J. Lyons and Company—the popular café and tea chain in Great Britain—bought a piece of land in Sudbury Mill, Middlesex, for a large sporting complex in honor of the 228 Lyons employees who had been killed in combat. On one edge, a twelve-foot, four-sided, nine-ton granite obelisk was constructed listing all the names. It was dedicated in 1922. After the World War II, a second memorial of Portland stone was constructed with the names of the 242 Lyons employees killed in that war. In the 1990s, the two monuments were moved to the Margravine Cemetery in Hammersmith, London.

The Great Western Railway honored the 2,524 employees killed in World War I by commissioning sculptor Charles Sergeant Jagger and architect Thomas S. Tait to create a memorial placed halfway along track one in Paddington Station. Sargeant created a larger than life-size solider cast in bronze. He is dressed in full battle gear with scarf and greatcoat, and he is reading a letter. *Soldier Reading a Letter* is placed within an architectural frame of white Portland stone. Unveiled on Armistice Day (November 11) in 1922, the interest in the memorial has recently been the subject of an imaginative digital and print project initiated by writers Neil Bartlett and Kate Pullinger. Their *Letter to an Unknown Soldier* website invited the public to imagine what the contents of the letter to the soldier might have been, creating "a new kind of war memorial" that allows the present generation to interact with the past.

REGIMENTAL MEMORIALS

The impressive *Royal Artillery Memorial* (1921-25) at Hyde Park Corner, London, is also the work of Charles Sargeant Jagger. A 9.2 inch Howitzer known as "Mother" is the central form of this monument. It is an enormous gun capable of throwing a 290-pound shell almost two miles. Modeled in stone, its barrel pointed to the sky, the ominous weapon is flanked on four sides by carefully modeled figures in bronze representing a dead soldier, an officer, a shell carrier, and an officer. Shallow-carved stone reliefs depict realistic scenes of trench warfare. The names of the battles in which the men of the Royal Artillery fought are incised in the memorial. "A royal fellowship of death" is inscribed beneath the dead soldier and a stone at the base reads: "BENEATH THIS STONE IS BURIED THE ROLL OF HONOUR OF THOSE WHOSE MEMORY IS PERPETUATED BY THIS MEMORIAL. THEY WILL RETURN NEVER MORE BUT THEIR GLORY WILL ABIDE FOREVER."

Controversy arose when the memorial was unveiled. Some thought that depicting a weapon was a glorification of war; others thought that the rendering of the Howitzer was a reference to the machine gun depicted in C.R.W. Nevinson's painting *La Mitrailleuse*. Jagger's memorial is one of his many images that speak to the consequences of war in specific terms. His work for the Imperial War Museum and related war memorials are testaments to his anti-war sentiments.

Francis Derwent Wood—the British sculptor who created the controversial work entitled *Canada's Golgatha* for

Above, Charles Sargeant Jagger, *Great Western War Memorial*, 1922. Paddington Station, London. (Photo by William Spooner)

Right, Charles Sargeant Jagger, *Royal Artillery Memorial*, 1921-25. London.

Detail, *Royal Artillery Memorial.*

Detail, *Royal Artillery Memorial.*

Canada's war memorials—was commissioned to create the *British Machine Gun Corps Memorial* in 1925. This memorial is located near Hyde Park Corner, and it is similar to Jaggers' *Artillery Memorial* with its juxtaposition of the human form with military ordnance. A bronze nude figure of a young male (almost identical in pose to Donatello's *David* from 1409) stands on a vertical granite pedestal on which are inscribed the words "ERECTED TO COMMEMORATE THE GLORIOUS HEROES OF THE MACHINE GUN CORPS WHO FELL IN THE GREAT WAR." Underneath and in smaller script is incised the following: "Saul hath slain his thousands, But David his tens of thousands." In back of the standing figure, an altar-like block shape supports two Vickers machine guns that have been bronzed and have laurel wreaths draped over their barrels.

Canadian Battlefields Memorial, Dury, c.1920s. France.

BATTLEFIELD MONUMENTS

The various Dominions of the British Empire were also determined to commemorate the major battles in which their soldiers were the principal combatants. The Canadian Battlefields Commission chose eight battle sites to commemorate: three in Belgium and five in France. All of the sites featured carefully chosen plant materials. Six of the sites included a single block of grey Canadian granite with inscriptions in English and French describing the events commemorated. The following words were inscribed around the base of each block: "HONOUR TO CANADIANS WHO ON THE FIELDS OF FLANDER AND OF FRANCE FOUGHT IN THE CAUSE OF THE ALLIES WITH SACRIFICE AND DEVOTION."

The American Battle Monuments Commission erected both battlefield memorials and monuments and chapels for the eight military cemeteries in Belgium and France. Amongst the distinguished architects engaged were Paul Cret, John Russell Pope, Ralph Adams Cram, and George Howe. Cret's Aisne-Marne Memorial at Château-Thierry (1926-1932) commemorates the American forces who fought at the second battle of the Marne in 1918. Cret's overt neo-classical architecture contrasts with the figurative sculpture representing France and the United States executed by Alfred Bottiau. The hilltop siting enhances the dramatic reading of the work. Cret's *Memorial Chapel Flanders Field Cemetery* at Waregem,

Belgium appropriated Greco-Roman architectural sources, specifically *The Tower of the Winds* from the Athenian agora dating c. 50 B.C. Cret's chapel sited at the center of the cemetery provided both a surface on which to inscribe the names of the missing and a focus for the graves marked by white marble crosses that surround it.

In addition to the prodigious number of public and private forms of monuments and memorials of commemoration from the mid-1800s to the mid 1900s, Canada, Great Britain, and the United States collectively needed to erect national memorials in their respective capitals. In the following chapter we will examine these sacred national sites and monuments in Ottawa, London, and Washington, DC.

Paul Cret, *Château-Thierry American Monument*, 1926-32. Château-Thierry, France.

Chapter Five

"Mementoes of the Fearful Struggle":[25] Photography and Commemoration

PHOTOGRAPHY WAS ONLY about twenty years old when the America Civil War brought photographs into common currency during wartime. Through ambro types, tin types, and *carte de visites*, this new method of recording history was just beginning to be a "peoples' art." What we have come to know as photo-*journalism* was only in its infancy in both the Civil War and World War I, even with a gap of fifty years between them. During both wars, the cameras were too cumbersome to safely lug around war zones. To expose a negative meant you had to expose yourself to enemy fire. No one hazarded it in the Civil War, and few did so in the First World War.

During the Civil War, newspapers and magazines were still sending out sketch artists to cover many actions. Such an artist could keep three or four sketches going on a pad simultaneously. He could "expose" his images anywhere and compress several actions into one sketch. Meanwhile, prominent photographers Matthew Brady, Alexander Gardner, Timothy O'Sullivan, and others set out with their bulky cameras, tripods, and portable darkrooms, setting up their photographic easel to paint with light and chemicals and fix images for eternity. For fifteen to thirty minutes they had to focus on one image entirely, from composition to final negative.

The starkness of black and white images lent a "relentless verity"[26] to the images, which set them off from the sketches and gave an added layer of verisimilitude. But this would soon fall prey to the practices of staged settings and fake images. Even early on in combat use, photography could be used for deception and indirection. Starkness and novelty might connote Truth, but context was vital.

As Peter Galassi has argued in an influential book on the history of photography, the change in perception of the world was a gradual process whereby the painters came to "value pictures that seem to be caught by the eye rather than composed by the mind. Photography… was born of this fundamental transformation in artistic value."[27] The congruence of photography and painting at mid-century was found in their common "formal strategies capable of suggesting the

---

25   Alexander Gardner. *Gardner's Photographic Sketch Book of the Civil War*. New York: Dover Publications, 1959.

26   *Ottawa Journal*, July 1917.

27   Peter Galassi. *Before Photography: Painting and the Invention of Photography*. New York: Museum of Modern Art, 1981.

immediacy and relativity of everyday life."[28] Nowhere was that commonality more apparent than in the skirmishes and battles of the Civil War, captured with kindred veracity by artists for *Harper's* and independent photographers.

"Emulsified Monuments": Gallery-style comparisons of the uses of photography

In the following sections, we aim to examine four uses of photography from the two wars. We have created an imaginary museum with four different galleries displaying the "emulsified monuments" of studio and battlefield. The first gallery presents officer portraits from both wars. The second describes two public exhibitions of mid-conflict war photographs. In the third, the changing views of photographic representation and manipulation are explored. In the last gallery, we come full circle and look at how photographs were turned into paintings.

Gallery I: The Dead to Be

Here are fifty or so photo portraits of officers killed in the two wars. None of the officers knew they would be dead, but surely they suspected it. The Vermont Civil War officers showed their photos to their family and friends. The British soldiers probably never showed their photos beyond friends, but after death, they were seen by hundreds of thousands.

Carte de visites (CDVs), miniature portraits used as calling cards, were extremely popular with soldiers and their families during the Civil War. These photographic calling cards, approximately 2.5 x 4 inches in size, had been invented in France in the early 1850s, and their popularity quickly spread throughout Europe and eventually to the United States. The carte de visites were relatively inexpensive. They became so popular that Oliver Wendell Holmes, Sr. wrote, "Card portraits ... have become the social currency, the 'green-backs' of civilization ... It seems as if nearly every one of the three million soldiers who took part in the war [had one]." This was a transitional moment in popular photography; instead of being only a novelty for the wealthy, photographs became available to everyone. It was not quite the "people's art of the 1880s" via Brownie cameras, but still a revolution. *Harper's* editor John Kouwenhoven later characterized the popularity of the medium as "living in a snapshot world.[29]"

Carte de visites were probably the first photographic images many of these officers ever had. They could have multiple copies, but the technology did not yet exist for the photos to be reprinted in local newspapers. The officers stood or sat, faced the camera or looked away. There was no spontaneity in the images, for the officers had to hold their poses for the several seconds needed to fix the image.

During most of the World War I, British weekly magazines such as *The London Illustrated News* and *The Graphic* published a "Roll of Honor," which was a page of photographs of officers recently killed. Some of these officers would likely

---

28   Ibid.

29   John Kouwenhoven. *Half a Truth is Better than None.* Chicago: University of Chicago Press, 1982.

Bartlett, Enoch H., 3rd VT INF, kia, Wilderness, 5/5/64

Beach, Watson Oakley, 5th VT INF, kia, Wilderness, 5/5/64

Bixby, Orville, 2nd VT INF, kia, Wilderness, 5/5/64

Converse, John Rollin, 14th VT INF, 17th VT INF, kia, Petersburg Mine, 7/30/64

Davenport, George Daniel, 5th VT INF, kia, Wilderness, 5/5/64

Darrah, Samuel, 10th VT INF, kia, Cold Harbor, 6/6/64

Dillingham, Edwin, 10th VT INF, kia, Winchester, 9/19/64

Stetson, Ezra, 10th VT INF, kia, Cold Harbor, 6/1/64

Duhigg, Dennis, 11th VT INF, 15th VT INF, kia, Winchester, 9/19/64

Sherman, Merritt Hoag, 11th VT INF, kia, Weldon Railroad, 6/23/64

Martin, William E., 13th VT INF, 17th VT INF, kia, Petersburg Mine, 7/30/64

Randall, George C., 1st VT INF, 6th VT INF, kia, Wilderness, 5/5/64

Carte de visites of twelve Vermont officers killed in the Civil War. Collection, Vermont Historical Society.

have gazed at previous "Halls of Honor." In this copy from October 1916, the war was in its third year. It was only four months after the bloodiest day in British military history—when 20,000 soldiers were killed on the first day of the Somme battle. Like the Civil War photos, these were privately taken. The magazines contacted the families of the deceased and asked permission to use their photo on a page like this. The magazines wanted to make the photos as appealing as possible; touchingly, they even printed the parents' names and home village. There was a certain symmetry in the layout on the page. But there was a certain *asymmetry* in the size of the photos to reflect the rank or station of the dead. Week after bloody week, the full-face cameos appeared—after the owners' bodies had been blown apart on the battlefield.

Gallery II: Graphic Shock and Awe

Here are works from two real gallery shows, one from each war, which were meant to provide a sort of visual "shock and awe" experience. They both were mounted well into their respective conflicts and contained images of very significant battles. Both "curators" were impresarios of their day: Matthew Brady, the Civil War photographer and Max Aitken, M.P., Canadian industrialist and newspaper magnate. Further, they each raised money—but for very different purposes. One earned lots of money for the photographer, the other was held to raise money to document the Canadian War effort.

In October 1862, Matthew Brady, perhaps the most famous photographer in the world, hung a sign outside this studio in New York City. It read "The Dead of Antietam." Over the next six weeks, 50,000 people crowded in to see the blasted bodies from what was to be the bloodiest one-day battle in American history. These wrenching images by Alexander Gardner and James Gibson (hired by Brady) were not just for display but also for sale. Were viewers drawn to the show in order to have a piece of living history? Was it curiosity? Was there a family connection to the battle? Were the buyers drawn to the macabre? We don't know.

Brady didn't show any of his numerous gun emplacements, lines of wagons, cityscapes, groups of officers, or stacks of equipment; he showed bloating bodies, blasted farmhouses, destroyed fences. An anonymous correspondent for *The New York Times* wrote a 2200-word review, excerpted here:

> The living that throng Broadway care little perhaps for the Dead at Antietam, but we fancy they would jostle less carelessly down the great thoroughfare, saunter less at their ease, were a few dripping bodies, fresh from the field, laid along the pavement. There would be a gathering up of skirts and a careful picking of way; conversation would be less lively, and the general air of pedestrians more subdued ... There is a confused mass of names, but they are all strangers; we forget the horrible significance that dwells amid the jumble of type ... Each of these little names that the printer struck off so lightly last night, whistling over his work, and that we speak with a clip of the tongue, represents a bleeding, mangled corpse..
>
> Mr. Brady has done something to bring home to us the terrible reality and earnestness of war. If he has not brought bodies

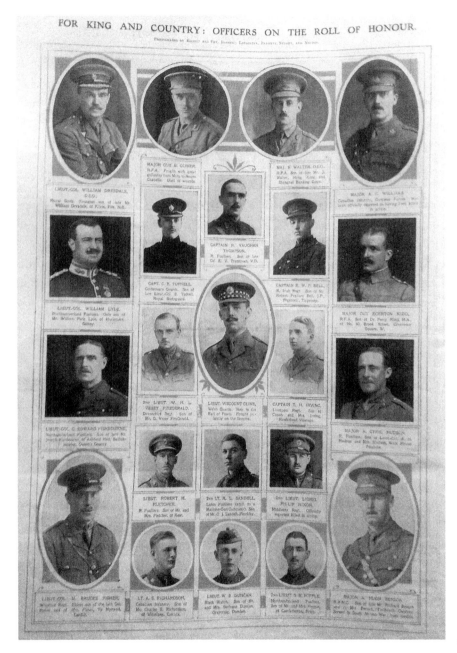

For King and Country, Officers on the Roll of Honor, October 21, 1916. (From the *London Illustrated News*)

Alexander Gardner, *Confederate Dead by Fence on Hagerstown Rd., Battle at Antietam*, September 1862. Library of Congress, Prints & Photographs Division, Civil War Photographs (LC-DIG-cwpb-01097)

Alexander Gardner, *Ditch on Right Wing, Battle of Antietam*, September 1862. Library of Congress, Prints & Photographs Division, Civil War Photographs (LC-DIG-ds-05184)

and laid them in our dooryards and along the streets, he has done something very like it … there is a terrible fascination about it that draws one near these pictures, and makes him loath to leave them. You will see hushed, reverent groups standing around these weird copies of carnage, bending down to look in the pale faces of the dead, chained by the strange spell that swells in dead men's eyes … there is poetry in the scene that no green fields or smiling landscapes can possess. Here lie men who have not hesitated to seal and stamp their convictions with their blood....

There is one side of the pictures that the sun did not catch, one phase that has escaped photographic skill. It is the background of widows and orphans, torn from the bosom of their natural protectors by the red remorseless hand of Battle, and thrown upon the fatherhood of God …

These pictures have a terrible distinctness. By the aid of the magnifying-glass, the very features of the slain may be distinguished … It was so nearly like visiting the battlefield to look over these views, that all the emotions excited by the actual sight of the stained and sordid scene, strewed with rags and wrecks, came back to us … [30]

The writer rubs the readers' noses in the "patriotic gore." He reminds them of the double-barreled human cost of

---

30 "Brady's Photographs. Pictures of the Dead at Antietam." *The New York Times,* Oct. 20, 1862.

blasted bodies and blasted families. But there is no question that the cause was worth the "knife" of sacrifice. The reviewer continues:

> *Yet through such martyrdom must come our redemption. War is the surgery of crime. Bad as it is in itself, it always implies that something worse has gone before. Where is the American, worthy of his privileges, who does not now recognize the fact, if never until now, that the disease of our nation was organic, not functional, calling for the knife, and not for washes and anodynes?*

It is unknown if Brady had any additional shows. Government censorship, primitive at first, then more sophisticated, made sure the public saw little of the carnage. By the end of the war, journalists and the Army had begun to play their cat and mouse game about what could be said or reported.

A second kind of show was mounted fifty-four years later during World War I by another kind of impresario, the Canadian Max Aitken, who was knighted as Lord Beaverbrook. He was not a photographer; he was a newspaper publisher. When Great Britain declared war on Germany on August 4, 1914, she also committed the peoples and resources of her global Empire to the fray: India, Australia, New Zealand, South Africa, Canada, and the rest. As Canadian Prime Minister Robert L. Borden noted, "The justice of the cause was recognized in every quarter of the King's Dominions, and nowhere more fully than in Canada."

An extremely successful businessman, Aitken had by his late twenties amassed a fortune in minerals and newspapers. He could also write quickly and fluidly. Appointed by Prime Minister Borden as Canada's "Official Eye Witness" to the front, with the honorary rank of Lieutenant Colonel, Aitken was determined to give a celebratory record of the Canadian Expeditionary Force overseas. Through his reporting, he would record the stories of many individual soldiers in his military diaries and documents. Portentously, he wrote, "I shall be content if one Canadian woman draws solace from this poor record of her dead husband's bravery." He would eventually write three books on the Canadians fighting in France.

As historian Maria Tippett observed, Aitken's position as Chief Records Officer "enabled him to roam freely about the Canadian lines … Canada had no war correspondents at the front, nor did Britain … Consequently the reports Aitken sent to England and Canada were unrivalled; they gave both countries a largely uncensored account of the performance of Canada's troops." [31]

The books were well received and sold well. But Aitken came to realize that his documentary reportage of the war effort could quickly get bogged down in the specifics of battle or of telling heroic stories. The bigger picture of the *Canadian* soldiers was not being depicted. To share this message, Aitken wanted some graphic punch. Illustrations in the two volumes of *Canada in Flanders* were limited to line drawings. Aitken now turned to the news media's emerging use of photography. He enlisted the services of two photographers who had been employed by London's *The Daily Mirror*:

---

31   Maria Tippett. *Art at the Service of War.* Toronto: University of Toronto Press, 1984. p. 18.

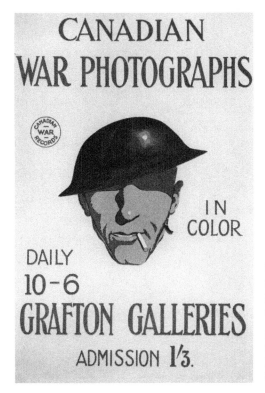

Left, advertisement, Grafton Gallery Exhibit of Canadian War Photographs, 1917. Collection, Canadian War Museum.

Right, advertisement, Grafton Gallery Exhibit of Canadian War Photographs, 1917. Collection, Canadian War Museum.

Harry Edward Knobel was appointed the first Official Canadian Photographer in the spring of 1916 and was replaced by William Ivor Castle six months later. A third photographer, William Rider, joined Castle in photo coverage of the war in June 1917.

The combined efforts of these Official War Records photographers resulted in three successful and popular exhibitions held in London between 1916 and 1919 and which circulated widely in Canada and the United States. We don't know if Beaverbrook or his aides ever heard of Brady's show. Nevertheless, in the intervening fifty years, censorship was so omnipresent that almost no photos of dead Canadians were shown. Indeed the subject matter was strikingly different.

Conventional newspaper photographs were small in scale, lacked legibility, and were short lived, owing to the fragile nature of the newsprint on which they were printed. The photographs exhibited by the Official War Records photographers were displayed as large-scale, oak-framed images, often hand tinted at the prestigious Grafton Galleries in London. This was the same gallery where artist Roger Fry and his coterie had assembled the Impressionist and Post-impressionist

Princess Christian looking at the Canadian Pictures Grafton Gallery London, 1917.
Canadian War Museum (CCO-CWM-FWWWP-260-EM-0142)

Ivor Castle, *The Garden of Sleep*. Canadian War Museum
(CCO-CWM-FWWWP-335-EM-0859c)

exhibitions, which had introduced modernist painting to English audiences several years earlier. The scale and manner in which the war photographs were displayed suggested that the works exhibited were viewed both as documentary and *artistic* images of the Great War.

There were hundreds of photos in the three exhibitions: giant artillery guns, liberated civilians, stretcher bearers, captured Germans, dead Germans, Red Cross teams, homing pigeons, etc. The mood most was cheerful and confident, and the catalogue captions were laced with bombast: "ARRAS: ALL THE HUNS HAVE LEFT OF THE ONCE BEAUTIFUL HOTEL DE VILLE: Before the Germans got to work this was one of the most stately town halls in France."

The dominant photo in the second exhibition was "The Taking of Vimy Ridge." At 11-by-20 feet, it was billed as the world's largest photograph. This battle in April 1917 was for Canada comparable to a combination of Saratoga, Gettysburg, and the Charge up San Juan Hill. The captions were effusive:

No individual soldier taking part in a modern battle can have the faintest idea of the scope of that battle...It is an

Ivor Castle, *The Taking of Vimy Ridge*, 1917.
Canadian War Museum (CCO-CWM-
FWWWP-263-EM-0262q)

awful pageant of War as it is waged today. It is an impression, nay indeed a reality, of the splendid horror of Vimy, snatched by the Photographer, in the fraction of a second, from the clutching of Death.

In fact, to make the Vimy horror even more "splendid," Ivor sandwiched three negatives together to show both the breadth of the scene and shells bursting overhead.

Copies of the displayed photographs were available for purchase in a variety of sizes, mounted or not. By all accounts, the exhibits were successful. The press loved the size and variety of the images. King George V and Queen Mary visited the first exhibition twice. Royalty and generals liked the plucky patriotic tone; the public loved the souvenirs they could buy. Admissions and photo sales from three shows brought in nearly $170,000 for the Canadian War Memorial project. As the *Ottawa Journal* noted in 1917, reviewing one of the duplicate exhibits: "There is a relentless verity about them that eats up the thousands of miles between Canada and the firing line, and brings a man to the brunt that the fellows are bearing."[32]

Photo historian Peter Robertson, in his essay on Canadian photojournalism during the First World War, gives a more nuanced conclusion, perhaps with the Brady show in mind:

> One senses that the collection shows photography coming to grips with twentieth century warfare, in the process losing much of the freedom and objectivity with which it had recorded such nineteenth century conflicts as the American Civil War, but also showing signs of foreshadowing the powerful photography which would later reveal the bloodshed, suffering and futility of the war in Vietnam.[33]

Gallery III: "A myth is what never was, and will always be."[34]

Here are two of the most famous, widely used war photographs of all time. They have appeared in countless anthologies and textbooks. In one lies the body of a Rebel sniper at Gettysburg, facing the camera, rifle draped across the body. In the other, plucky Canadian troops rise from their trenches to go "over the top," presumably amidst withering German fire, to march across no-man's land in World War I France.

Both images were staged.

It is easy to feel duped by this revelation. But ire can be melted into uneasy understanding by considering the liberty a painter might take with his or her subject. A painter would think nothing of rearranging elements for dramatic effect. Likewise, photography was beginning to establish its own rules for effect. As photography began to establish its own aesthetic, it turned out to have as many variables as painting. The moment a photographer first looks through a lens, he or she is making a choice, choosing a perspective. Through angle, use of light, framing, cropping—both at the instant of pressing the shutter and in the darkroom—the photographer had a wide range of impressions. It was only one step more to move the subject (or body, in this case) to get a more dramatic shot. Had Alexander Gardner stopped at the first sight of a collection of bodies and taken a picture, that would have shown one thing from one distance. But Gardner and other photographers changed their positions and angle to get a stronger photograph.

By the standards of the day, Gardner was "painting" with the body by moving it to a graphically more appealing spot.

---

32   *Ottawa Journal*, June 16, 1917. p. 18

33   Robertson, Peter. "Canadian Photojournalism during the First World War." *History of Photography* 2:1, Jan. 1978.

34   This quote from a sixth-century Bulgarian bishop in Robert Kaplan's book, *Balkan Ghosts* captured for me the enduring power of historical mythology. (St. Martin's Press, 1993)

Timothy O'Sullivan, *Home of a Rebel Sharpshooter,* 1863. Library of Congress, Prints & Photographs Division, Civil War Photographs (LC-DIG-ppmsca-33066)

Add a clean face, a clean rifle, a probably real setting, a proscenium of rocks. No one would criticize a painter who rearranged a body. In his further defense, Gardner was in a hurry. In the summer heat, the Union forces were trying to collect the bodies and bury them as quickly as possible.

But by today's standards, Gardner's sins were multiple. In his excellent photo-detective story *Gettysburg: A Journey in Time* William Frassanito exhaustively studied all of Gardner's images during that trip and concluded that Gardner had even used the same body in different photos in two different places forty yards apart.[35] Beside the body, he used a new rifle as a prop. He turned the face to the camera. The soldier was not even a sniper, and finally there are some hints that he used a negative from another photographer, Timothy O'Sullivan.

Captain Ivor Castle, an official Canadian photographer, was also in a hurry. He had to be covering battle scenes,

---

35   Frassinito, William. *Gettysburg: A Journey in Time*. New York: Charles Scribner's Sons, 1975.

Ivor Castle, *A Canadian Battalion Goes Over the Top"* Oct. 1916 Canadian War Museum CCO-CWM-FWWWP-041-EO-0874

Ivor Castle, *Over the Top,* another angle. (Courtesy Wikimedia Commons)

training exercises, and hospitals. Lord Beaverbrook and the War Records Office were hounding him and the others to get materials for shows for the "home folks." Castle didn't have to sell the photos to make his living, but he had to show the pluck and patriotism of the Canadian soldiers and prove that they are at least as brave as the British tommies. Getting actual shots of the fighting was difficult, almost impossible. A photographer could get killed just as easily as a soldier on the front lines. How best to show troops going "over the top?" One safe location was a training base at the village of St. Pol, well behind the front lines.

There, Castle got his shots of troops rising out of the trenches to come forward. No matter that one of the soldiers makes a face at the camera as he passes by. We can fix that in a caption which reads: "The Canadians making one of their brilliant attacks: men leaving their trenches on the Somme in high spirits." Then he took shots from the reverse side of the men getting out of the trenches up the slippery steep walls to march into a hail of bullets from the Germans. No matter that they had canvas covers on their rifles that render them inoperable. He fixed that with a diversionary tactic: he found some shell bursts from other pictures and sandwiched the images to give more drama. Then he added another caption that read: "… A German shrapnel bursting over a Canadian trench just as the Canadians are going over the parapet. A fragment of this shell killed the man whose body is seen sprawled across the parapet." In truth, the soldier had probably just slipped on the clay soil.

In an article for the publication *Canada in Khaki,* Castle gave no hint of his photographic license: "Nothing of course can be arranged. You sit or crouch in the front-line trench while the enemy do a little strafing, and if you are lucky you get your pictures." [36]

As Robertson, who later helped to expose this fakery, suggested, "The Canadian War Records Office tried, with a measure of success, to reconcile the nineteenth century belief that photography was an objective means of recording history, with the twentieth century fact that photographs were also a selective means of reinforcing the biases of official propaganda."[37]

Back to Paintings

In the final gallery is a sense that the genre has come full circle. We began with the historic transition from painting to photography; now we look at the use of photographs as sources for paintings in three pointed comparisons.

First Pairing: Harper's Weekly was the most widely viewed source of news during the Civil War. The magazine hired freelancers in addition to employing a staff of artists. They also bought photographs from Brady, Gardner, O'Sullivan and others, converting those images into line drawings. One of the most concentrated uses of such photographs was in a double-page spread of photographs from the battle of Antietam. (Some of the photos were ones Brady used in his Broadway show.) As photographs were not capable of being reproduced en masse at this time, Brady's macabre and grotesque images were transposed into a mechanically reproducible medium (wood engraving). The effect of the planar, somewhat abstract line-engraving distanced the viewer from the impact and immediacy of the original photograph—taking him one step further from the carnage.

Second Pairing: Looking at Gardner and Homer and thinking about their images, we sense how differently each medium conveys the grief of a fellow warrior. We can only speculate that Homer saw the original photograph, but we know that, as an artist for *Harper's*, he had witnessed what must sadly have been a common scene on the battlefield. There is obviously a similarity to the poses. Comparing the photos of Gardner at Antietam and the Houghton with the Homer drawing at the Fleming, each is effective at conveying the grief and carnage of the Civil War. Does it help to note that the Antietam photo shows the different treatment of a rebel soldier unburied and the grave of the Union dead? Does it make a difference how we view the subject, given the expressive qualities and aesthetic biases we might have for a drawing instead of a photograph, especially given the long and rich history of the graphic arts?

Third Pairing: On duty in France in 1918, the Canadian artist Fred Varley wrote to his wife:

> You in Canada … cannot realize at all what War is like. You must see it and live it. You must see the barren deserts war has made of once-fertile country… .see the turned-up graves, see the dead in the field, freakishly mutilated.

36   Ivor Castle. "With a Camera on the Somme" in *Canada in Khaki, A Tribute to the Officers and Men now serving in the Canadian Expeditionary Forces.* London (1917) p. 68.

37   Peter Robertson, "Canadian Photojournalism during the First World War," History of Photography, Vol. 2, Num. 1 January 1978, p. 51.

Battle of Antietam, drawings, October 18, 1862. (*Harper's Weekly*)

Alexander Gardner, *Photographs from the Battle of Antietam.* Library of Congress, Prints & Photographs Division, Civil War Photographs (LC-DIG-cwpb-04327; LC-DIG-cwpb-01095; LC-DIG-ds-05166; LC-DIG-ds-05186; LC-DIG-cwpb-03562)

The Battlefield After a Canadian Charge, October 1916. Canadian War Museum (CCO-CWM-FWWWP-044-EO-0940) A note reading "Not for sale or reproduction" appeared handwritten beneath the Canadian War Museum's print of this photograph.

Frederick Varley, *The Sunken Road,* 1919, oil on canvas. Collection, Canadian War Museum (#8912)

Headless, legless, stomachless, a perfect body and a passive face and a broken empty skull. See your own country-men, unidentified, thrown into a cart, their coats thrown over them; boys digging a grave in a land of yellow slimy mud and green pools of water under a weeping sky.

Propaganda had advanced enough so that photographs of dead Allies were almost always prohibited, although German dead were sometimes depicted. The pictures were marked "not for publication." However, as war art historian Laura Brandon points out, Canadian artist Fred Varley made significant use of some of those official photos when he painted dead bodies, which could be either German or Canadian, and then combined those with landscapes of his own experience.

Varley's painting *The Sunken Road* shows the direct use of an official photo. According to Brandon, Varley used the same photo image of the body in his painting of "German Prisoners." [38] But his artistic renderings in broad, textured brush

---

38   Laura Brandon. "Above or Below Ground? Depicting Corpses in First and Second World War Official Canadian Art" in *Bearing Witness: Perspectives on War and Peace from the*

work and a rich, colorful palette alters the black and white "matter of fact" impact of the photographic source and changes the content considerably. We can only speculate that people were seeing the painting before the photos. Did the bold colors of the painting distance the viewer from the starkness of the photograph? We could speculate endlessly on which is more powerful. That depends upon the audience, the timing, the display, the purpose.

As Beaverbrook was enjoying his public relations triumphs following the photography shows at the Grafton Galleries, he was dismayed to learn that the large-scale photographs, which he'd used so sensationally and successfully, had a limited shelf-life of only twenty-five years or so. Given his growing vision to use war art to build a Canadian national identity, he was determined that the proposed permanent collection should be of permanent materials, not gigantic photographs that faded before the viewers' eyes. The new national collection must have some big canvases to memorialize the great conflicts. Beaverbrook's answer, the Canadian War Memorial Project, under Konody's directorship, is the subject of our next chapter.

Arts and Humanities. Montreal: McGill-Queens University Press, 2012. p. 99. Brandon is adjunct professor in the School for Studies in Art and Culture at Carleton University, Ottawa, Canada.

CHAPTER SIX

Records, Propaganda, and Art: Lord Beaverbrook's War Memorials Projects

"The Great War was the first to be officially recorded by artists ... Art became a powerful weapon."
—A.E.Gallatin

"My obvious belief was that War was now dominated by machines and that men were mere cogs in the mechanism"
—C.R.W. Nevinson

THE THIRD SON of ten children born to a Presbyterian minister and his wife, William Maxwell Aiken was born in 1879 at Maple, Ontario. He was ambitious and eager to succeed. He bypassed university, taking what turned out to be a short-lived job as a journalist for *The Montreal Star* before being drawn into the world of finance. In a relatively short period of time Aitken garnered a reputation as a shrewd businessman. By 1910, he had moved to England and invested in the news-paper industry (*The London Globe* and *The Daily Express*). He soon became involved in politics, and with his considerable wealth, business connections, and political ambition, he secured a seat in the House of Commons representing Ashton Under Lyne. He financially supported the Conservative Party and in 1911 was knighted by King George V as Lord Beaverbrook. When the Great War broke out in the late summer of 1914, Beaverbrook's considerable influence and high profile as a Canadian-born member of Parliament led to his appointment by Canadian Prime Minister Robert Borden as Official Eyewitness for Canada. His task was to record and report the actions of the Canadian Expeditionary Force.

With his keen interest and successful background in journalism, Beaverbrook enthusiastically took on the task of documenting the daily activities and sacrifices of his fellow Canadians. By 1915 he had published *Canada in Flanders*, a detailed description of the principal battles in which the Canadians were engaged. As noted in the previous chapter, Beaverbrook also employed photographers whose photographs were exhibited at the prestigious Grafton Galleries in London. The exhibits were both a financial and popular success. While Beaverbrook did not deny the verity and power of the photographic image, he questioned its longevity. He came to believe that photographs "had a life span of only twenty-five years" and began to explore other possibilities for creating more permanent and lasting aesthetic records of Canada's

William Notman and Co., *Max Aitken, later Lord Beaverbrook,* 1905. Montreal,Quebec. McCord Museum, Montreal (II-156536)

Benjamin West, *The Death of General Wolfe*, 1770, oil on canvas. Collection, National Gallery of Canada (No.8807) Transfer from Canadian War Memorials, 1971.

role in the war.

In January of 1916, Beaverbrook was instrumental in creating the Canadian War Records (CWR) office. However, he soon found himself at odds with Canada's chief archivist and Keeper of Records Arthur Doughty. Doughty questioned Beaverbrook's ability to document Canada's war effort. Archives, for Doughty, were objective historical records. Beaverbrook, on the other hand, was neither archivist nor historian. He was a journalist. Soon after the CWR office was established, he developed an interest in exploring the possibilities of commissioning artists to chronicle the war, changing his approach to documenting Canada's war efforts from "objective record taking" to "subjective works of art."

There were precedents for turning to painting. War—its destruction and aftermath—had been a recurring subject of Western art history. While visiting the National Gallery of Art in London, Beaverbrook found a model for his proposed project: Paolo Uccello's *The Battle of San Romano,* 1438-40. The work was comprised of three panels forming a triptych. Each panel was roughly five and half feet by eight feet. Although decorative in style, Uccello's work created a visual record of an actual event: the 1432 battle between the armies of Florence and Sienna.

Eric Kennington, *The Kensingtons at Laventie*, 1915, oil on canvas. Collection, The Imperial War Museum, London.

C.R.W. Nevinson, *La Mitrailleuse*, 1915, oil on canvas. Collection, Tate, London (No.3177) Presented by the Contemporary Art Society, 1917. (Tate Images)

There were also historical paintings in private collections in England relating to war and to Canada's history which were known to Beaverbrook. Benjamin West's *The Death of General Wolfe, 1770*—the iconic history painting depicting the sacrificial death of the British general fatally wounded while securing the final victory of Great Britain over France in the struggle for North America—was owned by Beaverbrook's friend Hugh Grosvenor, Duke of Westminster. Grosvenor later presented the painting to Canada. At Beaverbrook's urging, other gifts and acquisitions were forthcoming, including Sir Joshua Reynolds 1765 portrait of *Sir Jeffery Amherst*; George Romney's 1776 portrait of *Joseph Brant [Thayendanegea]*; and portraits and watercolors pertaining to the early history of Canada. They offered further evidence for Beaverbrook's growing belief that painting could be an effective means of visually recording Canada's efforts in the Great War. And then there was the success and critical acclaim for the work of two contemporary British artists—widely divergent in style—who had documented the actions of the British Army at the Front in 1915: Eric Kennington's *The Kensingtons at Laventie*.

and C.R.W. Nevinson's *La Mitrailleuse*.

Kennington's painting was completed while he was recuperating from war service in 1915. A bleak winter scene in the small French town of Laventie shows a small group of exhausted British soldiers from the London Regiment resting, fresh from battle. The artist modestly portrays himself in the black balaclava in the left background of the composition. With sharp and photographically crisp details, the brilliantly colored reverse painting on glass contrasts sharply with contemporary war photographs of similar scenes: images limited in hue and range to black, white, and gray. The stiff, robotic positions of the individual soldiers further heighten the dramatic, stage-like presentation. When the painting was exhibited at the Goupil Gallery in 1916, critical praise for the painting helped to secure Kennington's later appointments as Official War Artist to both the British and Canadian projects.[39]

Stylistically distinct from Kennington's painting, C.R.W. Nevinson's La Mitrailleuse was cast in the contemporary avant-garde vocabulary of early cubism. Three faceless French soldiers, identifiable by their helmets and uniforms, operate a machine gun from a trench overhung with barbed wire. The angular and fractured forms create a mechanical analogue for the anonymity and destructive power felt by those at the Front. Also exhibited in London in 1916 at the Grafton Galleries (March) and Leicester Galleries (September-October), the painting was purchased by the Contemporary Art Society later that year. Walter Richard Sickert, one of England's most revered senior painters, declared that La Mitrailleuse was the "most authoritative and concentrated utterance of war in the history of painting. This must be for the nation."["O Matre Pulchra", Burlington Magazine, XXlX, 1916.p.35] The Contemporary Art Society presented the painting to the Tate Gallery in 1917.

The success of these artists would have been noted by Beaverbrook, and the public attention that their work drew probably influenced Parliament's vote in 1917 to establish an Imperial War Museum based on a proposal by First Commissioner of Works Sir Alfred Mond. Materials to be collected and displayed for the proposed museum were to include both civilian and military documents representative of the sacrifices of all who were involved in the war effort. Mond and Charles Masterman, the head of the British War Propaganda Bureau, had already begun to recruit artists and writers in 1916, creating a unique government patronage of the arts. Masterman understood the limitations of "pictorial propaganda" restricted solely to film and photography. As Meirion and Susie Harries later observed[The War Artists, 1983,p.7]

> "... Illustrated publications [from Wellington House] depended on a steady flow of suitable photographs which in 1916 was difficult to sustain. There were too few official photographers on the Western Front and too limited a range of subjects: the flat empty landscapes of Flanders, trench scenes, numberless troops going 'over the top'

---

39   It is conceivable that it was Kennington's painting that prompted Wyndham Lewis, the outspoken leader of the abstract Vorticist movement in London, to observe: "There is no reason why very fine representational paintings of the present War should not be done."

and so on … .the decision to use artists rather than illustrators or cartoonists to supply the badly needed pictures was actually taken by Masterman himself."

By early 1916, Masterman had commissioned British artists Muirhead Bone and Francis Dodd to go to France to document war activities. Their work was such a success that within a year, Eric Kennington, William Orpen, Paul Nash, C.R.W. Nevinson, and William Rothenstein were also appointed and sent to the Front. The aim of the British War Propaganda Bureau was clear: to inform, to persuade, and to propagate by visual means the government's support for the war effort, both abroad—especially in America—and at home. The results of Masterman's scheme form the body of what has come to be known the British War Memorials project.

Beaverbrook borrowed the British War Propaganda Bureau's model of commissioning artists to record wartime activities for a similar project documenting the war efforts of the Canadians. In November 1916, Beaverbrook assembled several close friends to form the Canadian War Memorials Committee. Beaverbrook was a sitting member, Newspaper magnate Harold Harmsworth (Lord Rothermere) was chairman, and Captain Bertrand Lima from the Canadian War Records Office was also involved. In a diplomatic move, the Chairman of the Board of Trustees for the National Gallery of Canada, Sir Edmund Walker, was appointed advisor to the committee to insure that Canadian artists would be adequately represented.

The Canadian War Memorials Committee was officially recognized in 1917. The funding was provided by the sale of official photographs and books published by the Canadian War Records Office: *Canada in Flanders, Canadian War Pictorial*, and *Canada in Khaki*. The goal of the memorials was to commission pictures by well-known contemporary artists which would be a visual record of Canada's efforts in the Great War; an enterprise distinct from the writings and publications of the Canadian War Records Office. With the creation of the Canadian War Memorials scheme, Beaverbrook's eyewitness role shifted from the creation of objective archival war records to propagating the efforts of Canadians at home and abroad by commissioning works of art by contemporary British and Canadian artists.

II

"Commissions for decorative paintings on a heroic scale were distributed among artists of every creed, from the ultra-conservative Academician to the revolutionary vorticist, care being taken in every case to secure the best representation of every school of artistic thought and to find for each subject the artist most likely to do justice to it."—Paul George Konody

Beaverbrook's Committee chose Paul George Konody as artistic advisor to develop and to oversee the project. He was well suited to the task. Konody was a widely published art historian, was knowledgeable about Italian and Flemish Renaissance art, and had recently authored a monograph on C.R.W. Nevinson. The most important of his credentials for Beaverbrook was his familiarity with the contemporary art scene in London. He was art critic both for *The Observer* and *The Daily Mail*, the latter paper owned by Beaverbrook's close friend Lord Norhcliffe. Konody's aim was "to make the CWM collection … truly representative of the artistic outlook during the momentous period of the Great War." To achieve this ambitious goal, he argued that work "representative of every step leading from strictly representation to abstract art" in the visual arts needed to be included.[40] He identified eleven distinct stylistic "tendencies" which he listed as academic, realist, naturalist, *plein air*-istes, impressionists, neo-realists, neo-impressionists, expressionists, cubists, vorticists, and futurists. Because of Konody's inclusive approach, the CWM became both an encyclopedic survey of contemporary British and Canadian art as well as a narrative view of Canada's participation in the First War. So many British artists were invited to participate in the CWM that they joked they were really members of the "Konodian Army." Sir Alfred Munnings, one of the many British artists hired by Konody, recalled a poem offered at a dinner in Konody's honor at the Café Royal in London: "I'm a judge of ancient and modern Art/In Art I take the leading part./Of a great concern I am the start;/For I am the brain, the mind, the heart/Of the great Konodian Army."

The battles in which the Canadians fought, especially Corcellette and Vimy, would leave 60,000 Canadian troops dead. And this after four long years of protracted warfare. Battle scenes were first in the list of subjects Konody proposed to be rendered in paint. The war had created wastelands strung with wire, carved by trenches, and unearthed and muddied by shellfire. Flooded by constant rain, the battlefields were strewn with the flotsam and jetsam of war; dead bodies haphazardly mingled with corpses of animals and the destroyed machinery of modern warfare. Was it possible for an artist to capture the dizzying and painful effects of mustard gas experienced by Canadian soldiers at Ypres? Depicting such horrors in a convincing visual language was a challenge artists had not faced before. British artist William Roberts, a member of the Vorticist coterie before the war, succeeded in meeting that challenge in his vigorously expressive *First German Gas Attack at Ypres* of 1918. A cacophony of color and angular form, the picture convincingly embodied what Canadian Prime Minister Robert Borden observed about mustard gas in 1915: "[It is] an unknown and terrible means of warfare … poured upon them: torture and death."

British artist Eric Kennington's *The Conquerors*—originally entitled *The Victims*—was also compelling in its depiction of the "torture and death" of which Borden spoke. Kilted Canadians of the Sixteenth Battalion, some depicted as vapor-like ghost, were seen by the artist as victims rather than as conquerors. It was an observation that would be echoed by many of the war poets as well. One reviewer of Kennington's painting claimed it as "the finest war picture painted. It is

---

40   Konody, Paul George. "On War Memorials" from *Art and War*. London: Canadian War Records Office, 1919.

William Roberts, *The First German Gas Attack at Ypres*, 1918. Collection, National Gallery of Canada (No.8729) Transfer from Canadian War Memorials,1971.

relentless, it is truthful, and it is filled with great beauty."[41] Others saw its meaning as ambivalent; its pre-surrealist-based composition, ambiguous forms, and jarring palette having neither the clarity nor power of his earlier work.

There were also paintings of non-combative soldiers who faced the day to day drudgery of war. Canadian artist James Wilson Morrice's painting *Canadians in the Snow* depicts a contrary view to Kennington's. A light snow is falling as Canadian infantry trudge along a country road past a windmill. Toy-like airplanes cavort in the sky. The forms are rendered in broad shapes, and a simple palette creates an impression of a quiet, pastoral landscape removed from war.

As the project developed, Konody expanded his goals, commissioning Canadian and British artists to capture the efforts of Canadian civilians involved in the war effort at home. He asked for images of munitions workers in Toronto, sawyers cutting spruce for airplanes in British Columbia, young men in training camps in Petawawa, Ontario, agricultural workers sowing and harvesting crops, and troop ships in dazzling camouflage embarking from Halifax harbor. The staging

---

41   *American Art News,* Nov.15, 1920.

Eric Kennington, *The Conquerors,*1920, oil on canvas. Collection, Canadian War Museum (No.0812)

James Wilson Morrice, *Canadians in the Snow*, 1918. Oil on canvas. Collection, Canadian War Museum. No.0805.

of Canadian troops in England at training camps such as Seaford, Ripton, and Whitley, the wounded and battle-exhausted soldiers resting behind the lines in France, as well as those recuperating in hospitals back in England were also part of Canada's epic narrative—as were the men and women who received services provided by the Red Cross and YMCA.

Konody's final scheme incorporated twenty subjects as the basis for the Canadian War Memorials narrative. He assigned specific subjects to artists whom he felt best suited to the task. Sir William Orpen was assigned to paint portraits of the Victoria Cross honorees while Sir Alfred Munnings painted the horse-riding cavalry subjects. There were also commissioned artists whose work was of a more symbolic nature. Charles Sims' *Sacrifice* is a striking allegory, the subject alluding in both general and specific ways to the tragedies of the death of young men and the loss experienced by their families. Sims' eldest son had been killed in the first year of the war. Seen from the vantage point of a spectator (the artist) in back of the Crucifixion (the artist's son) the immediate foreground (displaced civilians) and background (injured soldiers) contrast different kinds of sacrifice made by men and women whose lives are overturned by war. The top of the painting is edged with badges and emblems of the Canadian Forces.

Viewing the overall scheme, one might conclude that Konody rejected visual cohesiveness for structural logic, en-

Charles Sims, *Sacrifice*, 1918, oil on canvas. Collection, Canadian War Museum (No.0662)

couraging the Canadian War Memorials to be read as a well-constructed book. Each "chapter" was punctuated by a large scale painting—forty in all—exceeding eight feet in at least one dimension and functioning as radiating spokes from a monumental mural twelve feet high and forty feet in length which was to be the central hub and focal point of the scheme.

The subject of this mural-size narrative painting was the Canadian Expeditionary Force (CEF) resting after the heroic Battle of Vimy Ridge (all four divisions of the CEF had participated). Prisoners of war and refugees are assembled in the small French town of Lens. The commission was given to acclaimed British artist and figurative painter Augustus John. Variously titled *The Canadians Opposite Lens* or *The Pageant of War*, John's painting was divided into eight contiguous segments—each twelve feet high and five feet wide—totaling forty feet in length. Several sketches for the unfinished paint-

Augustus John, *Canadians Opposite Lens*, 1920, oil on canvas. Collection, Canadian War Museum, Ottawa (No.001)

ing show a *tableau vivant* stretched across the foreground of a ruined landscape of buildings and trees with disparate groups of soldiers, including cavalry, interspersed with displaced civilians. A lone roadside crucifix is inserted amidst the clutter in the right middle ground; a toy-like dirigible floats into the left side of a cloudy sky. The procession of figures belies any apparent compositional scheme; no plausible narrative holds the work together.

The war ended before John could complete what would have been his most ambitious work. The artist later admitted he was discouraged from finishing because the war museum Beaverbrook had proposed for Ottawa (for which the painting was intended) was never realized. John referred to this commission as his "Canadian incubus." An oil sketch, roughly one foot by four feet, titled *Canadians at Lievin Castle* was acquired by the Beaverbrook Art Gallery in Fredericton, New Brunswick. The partially complete oil cartoon for the full-scale painting held in a private collection was discovered in 1994 and was acquired by the Canadian War Museum in Ottawa in 2011.

Konody and Beaverbrook were both also working with the British War Memorials Committee (BWMC), which was established in March of 1918. The members included Beaverbrook, Arnold Bennett, Charles Masterman, and Alfred Yockney. Konody again served as artistic advisor. The BWMC followed the Canadian model, commissioning fifteen British artists to execute large paintings—six-by-ten foot canvases—documenting various activities of the British Army. Many of the artists employed had also worked for the Canadian War Memorials scheme: Wyndham Lewis, William Roberts, and Paul Nash among the best known. The large paintings would also frame a monumental mural—a commission given to the distinguished American artist John Singer Sargent. Together, the paintings and mural would form a "Hall of Remembrance" for the proposed Imperial War Museum.

Sargent's large-scaled mural entitled *Gassed* measured seven and a half feet high by twenty feet in length, and was

John Singer Sargent, *Gassed*, 1919, oil on canvas. Collection, Imperial War Museum, London.

completed in March 1919. The subject was proposed by David Lloyd George; he suggested the work convey the collaboration of British and American forces. The painting illustrates British and American soldiers suffering from exposure to mustard gas led in a line by an orderly across a duck walk to a makeshift hospital tent. A group of soldiers play soccer in the background. The artist's juxtaposition of the healthy with the wounded might be interpreted as a comment critical of those who would see war as merely sport—a "good rugger game." It is unique among the British and Canadian War Memorial commissions in its acknowledgement of the role of the American Expeditionary Force in the Great War.

Sargent's compositional format and historical allusions to Brueghel's *Blind Leading the Blind* (1568) and Gericault's *Raft of the Medusa* (1818) together create a powerful and compelling image of the horrors of war and the helplessness of those wounded by it. Interestingly, Sargent was familiar with John's CWM mural, recording his impressions after viewing the preliminary oil sketch at a later exhibition:" I have just come from the Canadian Exhibition where there is a hideous post-impressionist picture of which mine [*Gassed*] cannot be accused of being a crib ... Augustus John has a canvas forty feet long done in his free and script style. But without beauty of composition."[42] In both the Canadian and British schemes, the large murals of Augustus John and John Singer Sargent intertwine scale and content, presumably to convey the meaning, or lack thereof, of a war that's magnitude and destruction had dragged on for four years.

---

42   Quoted from Michael Holroyd's *Augustus John:* Vol II, 1975, p.73

III

When the war finally ended in the fall of 1918, many of the works commissioned for the Canadian War Memorials had not been completed. Over the next several years, exhibitions of the CWM were held in London and in major cities in North America with additional works added as the paintings were finished. The reviews of the traveling exhibitions were mixed. A press release for the 1919 American viewing of the Canadian War Memorials at the Anderson Galleries in New York at 59th and Park Avenue summarized the Canadian scheme as "A series of decorative panels ... thought out in connection with an architectural scheme ... to form a suitable and imposing framework ... so that they will present themselves as an impressive ensemble in orderly sequence." "Decorative panels" in "orderly sequence" did not adequately summarize what Konody and Beaverbrook had achieved. The use of terms like "decorative" and "decoration" when applied to works of art whose subject was war was confusing to many. In an accompanying publication to the exhibits—*Art and War: Canadian War Memorials,* co-authored with Percy Godenrath— Konody's use of the term "decorative" was difficult for the average viewer to comprehend. Describing Wyndham Lewis' *Canadian Gunpit,* Konody wrote:

> The terraced group of figures among shells are not intended to be anything but rugged in the matter of physiognomy. The painting is furthermore a decoration, essentially, and its treatment subordinates to the great lines of balance and arrangement-the impressionistic truth of modern pictorial art. It is an experiment of the painter's, a kind of painting not his own.

His description led the viewer to believe that Lewis' painting was both a historical record of a specific time, place, and event, and an aesthetically significant example of modern "decorative" art. Was the work capable of accomplishing both goals, or did it fall short of being either?

The overall stylistic and aesthetic language of the memorial projects was as broad and diverse as the artists commissioned for the project; but it was clear that Konody was not neutral in his aesthetic preferences. Although he commissioned Augustus John to execute the central mural in a figurative and somewhat academic style, the older artistic idioms for Konody could not "adequately express the grim hard, mechanical character" of modern warfare. Only in the often quite intelligible experiments of Cubism and Futurism could be found the germ of such an idiom.[43] Lewis's work and a handful of paintings by British and Canadian artists embodied for Konody what historian Paul Fussell characterized as

---

43   Konody, "On War Memorials," Op. cit.

Wyndham Lewis, *A Canadian Gunpit,* 1918, oil on canvas. Collection, National Gallery of Canada (No.8356) Transfer from Canadian War Memorials, 1971.

the "paranoid melodrama" which extended trench warfare created.[44]

There were other British artists—Paul Nash, William Roberts, Frederick Etchells, Edward Wadsworth, and David Bomberg—who also successfully experimented with new and convincing ways to depict the horrors, confusion, anonymity, and chaos of mechanized warfare. In the case of Bomberg, his abstract rendering of the subject, *Sappers at Work,* was rejected by Konody and the Committee. A more figurative second version was finally accepted by the CWM.

When finally completed, the Canadian War Memorials numbered some eight hundred works, among them paintings, watercolors, lithographs, etchings and sculptures. Three-dimensional work comprised a very small part of the CWM project. Only Ivan Mestrovic's powerful sculptural relief, *Canadian Phalanx,* succeeded in giving sufficient expression to the mechanized and anonymous aspect of the war. Derwent Wood's bronze relief entitled *Canada's Golgatha,* 1918—figurative in style—proved the more controversial because of its subject: the purported crucifixion of a Canadian solider by

---

44   From his seminal book, *The Great War and Modern Memory* (Oxford University Press, 1975).

Edward Wadsworth, *Dazzle Ships in Drydock at Liverpool*, 1919. Collection, National Gallery of Canada (No.8925) Transfer from Canadian War Memorials, 1971

David Bomberg, Study for *Sappers at Work, A Canadian Tunneling Company, Hill 60, St. Eloi*, c.1918-1919. Collection, Tate Gallery, London (No.T00319 at Tate Images)

the enemy.

Several decades later, many of the works of the CWM were not forgotten, Sir Kenneth Clark recorded the effect of the Canadian War Memorials exhibition he had seen at the Royal Academy of Arts in London in 1919:

> The impact of this exhibition was unforgettable … there appeared two huge and uncompromising examples of Vorticism. William Roberts's "Gassed Man" [*First German Gas Attack at Ypres*] and Wyndham Lewis's "Gun Pit" [*A Canadian Gunpit*] It was the first time that the harsh voice of the twentieth century had been heard within the walls

David Bomberg, *Sappers at Work, A Canadian Tunneling Company*, 1919, final version. Collection, National Gallery of Canada, Ottawa. Transfer from Canadian War Memorials, 1971.

of the Royal Academy…The canvasses of Roberts and Lewis had, on the few visitors who took them in, the same effect of liberating shock that the *Demoiselles d'Avignon* had produced in Paris ten years earlier… Augustus John, whose cartoon of Canadian Soldiers at Lens[Canadians Opposite Lens] filled the whole end of Gallery III, was considered very advanced….Paul Nash remains the hero of the occasion. His poetic recreations of front line desolation, although pictorially a little thin, are genuinely moving and convincing… indeed, if one allows one's mind to reflect on an aesthetic image of the 1914-18 war, it will almost certainly take the form of a Paul Nash.[45]

Canadian artists were not as familiar as were their British counterparts with the new futurist/cubist language of pre-war Europe, but they did create powerful and convincing images of war—as can be seen in the works of Fred Varley, A.Y. Jackson, and many others. The exposure of these Canadian artists to contemporary European and British art, plus their shared experience of the horrors of war impacted their post-war paintings. Upon their return to Canada, F.H. Varley and his contemporaries created bold new landscape im-

---

45   Clark, Sir Kenneth. "Introduction" from *The War Artists*. Folkestone Gallery, 1964.

Ivan Mestrovic, *Canadian Phalanx*, 1920. Ottawa.

Derwent Wood, *Canada's Golgatha*, 1918. Collection, Canadian War Museum,Ottawa (No.0797)

ages which both echoed and extended the earlier twentieth-century primal visions of Tom Thomson's Algonquin Park paintings and A.Y. Jackson's pre-war masterpiece, *La Terre Sauvage*. These expressive post-war images-nationalist in their iconography- envisioned a starker, untouched northern wilderness of the Canadian Shield— a vision contrasting with the agricultural landscape of Europe ravaged and destroyed by war.

IV

"In addition to their historical and national significance, there is no doubt that these War Memorials constitute one of the foremost collections of modern British and Canadian art in existence."—Eric Brown, 1926

The CWM were formally transferred to the Canadian Government in the fall of 1920, but Beaverbrook's proposal to

F.H.Varley, *Stormy Weather, Georgian Bay,* 1920, oil on canvas. Collection, The National Gallery of Canada, Ottawa (No.1814)

A.Y. Jackson, *La Terre Sauvage ,*1913, oil on Canvas. Collection. The National Gallery of Canada, Ottawa.

build a war museum (designed by the distinguished British architect E.A. Rickards) to house the collection was rejected by the Canadian government. The government had little money or desire to fund such a proposal. It was too costly, too "Edwardian Baroque." Prime Minister McKenzie King had other priorities, the first of which was to make Ottawa live up to her name architecturally as the Capital of Canada. When King assumed office in 1921, the population of Ottawa was just over 150,000. It was decidedly not a burgeoning metropolis like Paris, London, or Washington, D.C. The Centre Block of the Parliament buildings was still under construction; the National Commemorative War Monument had just been commissioned; and the Nurses National Memorial by sculptor G.W. Hill of Montreal had won approval to be placed in the Hall of Honour in the newly rebuilt Centre Block. For King, it was enough to have eight of the largest and least visually controversial Canadian War

Memorial paintings hung on the wall of the senate chamber. The remaining Canadian War Memorials were placed under the care of the trustees of the National Gallery of Canada.

Eric Brown, the first director of the National Gallery of Canada, argued for a more permanent and spacious facility than the multi-functioned Victoria Museum to house both the existing collections of that institution and the War Memorials. Brown believed that the War Memorials deserved "to be exhibited for all time to come." But his dream of such a facility—like Beaverbrook's proposal for a national war museum—never materialized within his lifetime. For the next fifty years various proposals were forthcoming, but it was not until 1988 that architect Moshe Safdie's stunning post-modern building was finally constructed to house the collections of the National Gallery of Canada. By then, the CWM collections had been dispersed under the directorship of Jean Boggs. The significant examples of contemporary Canadian and British art were housed at the National Gallery of Canada; works of a more documentary nature and of large scale that were not placed on the walls of the senate chamber were transferred to the Canadian War Museum, a facility that was finally built in 2005 and was designed by the firm of Moriyama and Teshima.

The British, however, were successful in creating a national war museum (The Imperial War Museum) before war's end. As Martin Conway, director-general of the National War Museum argued before the War Cabinet as the rationale for such an institution:

> When peace returns and men are back at home the years will pass and memory of the great days and adventures [sic] through which they lived will grow dim. It is the purpose of the Museum to be a place which they can visit with their comrades, their friends, or their children, and there revive the past and behold again the great guns and other weapons with which they fought.

But the proposed Hall of Remembrance—a separate structure designed by Charles Holden—was never built. The paintings intended for Holden's proposal are now incorporated in the collections of the Imperial War Museum.

The works of art commissioned by the British and Canadian governments represent the most comprehensive art collections documenting the Great War. Much of the credit for the initial vision and the development of those collections belongs to Lord Beaverbrook, who came to understand the distinction between war records, propaganda, and works of art. Those distinctions today are iterated by the fact that both in Canada and in Great Britain, many of the "best" works of art commissioned for those schemes are displayed in National Art Museums as prime examples of "modern" art, and the remainder sequestered to the war museums.

CHAPTER SEVEN

Living Memorials

"For the whole earth is the sepulcher of famous men, and their story is not graven only on stone in their native earth, but lives on far away, without visible symbol, woven into the stuff of other men's lives."—Thucydides

"The culture of memorialization resembles a delta in which the demands of many groups and commemorative practices compete uneasily."—A. Shanken

MEMORIAL AUDITORIUM IN Burlington, Vermont—the city's largest civic performance arena—is not a thing of beauty. It looks like the inside of a kiln with its burnt bricks on the outside. The windows haven't been cleaned in decades, perhaps because most events held there occur mostly at night. It abuts Burlington's Central Fire Station from the same era and the modern addition to the Carnegie-endowed Fletcher Free Library.

In its eighty-five years, it has hosted rock bands and symphony orchestras, Bob Dylan, Marcel Marceau, Golden Gloves boxing tournaments, large-screen films, a semi-pro basketball team, variety shows, political rallies, and farmers' markets. It has permanent seating in the balcony, roll-out rows in the walls, and hundreds of temporary folding chairs that can fill the floor. The basement has a kindergarten and an art school and a small theater for youth rock bands. On the second floor, a drumming troupe practices several times a week; their sound—like steady rain—bounces off the walls of the telephone company building and the Congregational church nearby.

When it was dedicated in 1928, Mayor C.H. Beecher wrote in the *Burlington Free Press*, "Burlington now claims the largest and best equipped auditorium in New England north of Springfield, Mass., and is making a successful bid as the leading convention city of northern New England."

On the outside east wall is bolted an oxidized and almost illegible brass plaque, which reads:

Memorial Auditorium, 1928. Postcard.
Burlington, Vermont.

MEMORIAL AUDITORIUM
Dedicated 1928
By the City of Burlington
IN MEMORY OF ITS CITIZENS WHO WERE IN THE
MILITARY OR NAVAL SERVICE DURING WARS
IN WHICH THE UNITED STATES HAS BEEN ENGAGED

Burlington's civic auditorium was one of dozens, perhaps hundreds, of civic structures built as part of the an informal "living memorial" movement that arose in the United States after World War I. There was no national commission or government agency sending out packets of admonitory or celebratory verbiage. There were no templates of "how-to" in civic magazines. But there was a widespread feeling that in addition to erecting a plethora of "doughboy" statues and stone piles, municipalities should honor the veterans with useful objects that would both honor the dead and serve the living by promoting encounters, rituals, and pilgrimages. Contemplation was out; participation was in. Use would trump reverence and awe. The term "living monument" became applicable.

The earliest use of the term seems to be within a letter written by a Civil War veteran who had lost an arm in the conflict. Speaking for all the amputees, he wrote, "We are the living monuments of the late cruel and bloody Rebellion. We

Karl Gerhardt, *General George Stannard*, c.1890. Lakeview Cemetery, Burlington, Vermont.

now retire from field of blood and carnage to prepare to act another part in the great 'drama' of life."[46]

While many memorial buildings are public affairs, some are private donations to a community. Such a one is the Memorial Hall in Wilmington, Vermont. At the turn of the twentieth century, Major Frederick W. Childs, a Civil War hero and Wilmington's richest citizen, grew worried about how to honor his fellow Vermont Civil War veterans—then dying at an increasing rate. He hired Stanford White, of the famed New York architecture firm McKim, Mead and White, to design Childs' Tavern and then a theater to provide entertainment to the tourists and a gathering place for citizens. In his words, Memorial Hall was intended to foster "innocent diversion from the more exacting things of life" and to "always inspire the highest, broadest and sweetest sentiment in this community."

In Great Britain after World War I—although there was no living memorial movement, per se—the contemplation of over one million war-dead moved some to rebuke bitterly society's investment in traditional monuments. As the English architectural critic William Lethaby wrote, "Above all things, the returned soldiers, or their widows and mothers when they return no more, need houses. Would not a pleasant, tidy little house in every village bearing on a panel, MEMORIAL COTTAGE, and other words and names, be the most touching, significant, and beautiful of all possible monuments? The people asked for houses and we have given them stones."[47]

A less strident view was expressed at the annual meeting of the Managers of the New York Botanical Society in October, 1919:

Resolved: That the most effective and economical way to honor the war dead was to plant memorial trees ... Such trees may properly be

46   Jordan, Brian Matthew. "Living Monuments": Union Veteran Amputees and the Embodied Memory of the Civil War." Civil War History 57.2 (2011): 121-152. *Project MUSE.* Web. 20 Jul. 2014.

47   Lethaby, William Richard. *Form in Civilization; Collected Papers on Art & Labour,* London: Oxford Univ. Press, 1922. p. 65

McKim, Mead and White, *Memorial Hall*, 1902. Wilmington, Vermont.

planted in the front yard, on the street, at the home entrance, in a park, as the decoration of an avenue, in single specimens or in groups of different species for artistic effects of form and color. As representing sentiments to be long cherished, such memorials would be tenderly cultivated and protected …

In the two decades after World War I, scores of American cities and states added "Memorial" to the names of countless bridges, roadways, parks, libraries, playgrounds, community centers, civic auditoriums, and athletic fields to honor armies, military units, and individuals.[48] These new spaces were places for gatherings and performances. Grand stadiums were erected, such as Soldier Field in Chicago and Veterans Stadium in Philadelphia.

Universities were not to be outdone. Huge football stadiums rose on campuses in Kansas, Illinois, California, Oklahoma, Michigan, Texas, and elsewhere. Memorial Stadium in Champlain-Urbana was built in 1923 as a memorial to Illinois men and women who gave their lives for their country during World War I. Their names appear on 200 columns that support the east and west sides of the stadium. The stadium was dedicated officially October 18, 1924, when, in a 39-14 vic-

---

48   In 1934, following the annual Encampment of the Grand Army of the Republic veterans, the U.S. Government designated U.S. Route 6 the main (pre-Interstate) cross-country road the Official Grand Army of the Republic Highway.

Memorial Stadium, October 18, 1924. University of Illinois Champlain-Urbana (Photo courtesy of University of Illinois Department of Athletics)

tory over Michigan, Illinois' legendary Harold E. "Red" Grange accounted for six touchdowns, a record that stands today.

Municipalities followed suit with their own versions of living memorials. One grandiose project was the War Memorial Complex in San Francisco. There, city officials played to both military and civilian constituencies by building two structures—a Veterans Hall and a War Memorial Opera House. In 1945, many of the plenary sessions of the nascent United Nations took place in the Veterans Building. The actual signing of the U.N. Charter occurred in the Opera House, with President Harry Truman presiding.

In a fervor of patriotism and civic boosterism, leaders in Indianapolis reserved five blocks of the downtown for the development of memorials to the veterans of World War I. (It was not as if they had short-changed the Civil War: Indianans had already built the 284-foot tall Sailors and Soldiers Monument in the city center.) The area was aligned with the urban planning concepts of the City Beautiful movement of the period. The new plan consisted of a main memorial and two auxiliary buildings, an obelisk, a mall, and a cenotaph. In addition, they enticed the newly formed American Legion to move its national headquarters from St. Louis to the city.

A second wave of aversion to fixed monuments arose during and after World War II. The critic Andrew Shanken describes a domestic battle over war memorializing as a "sometimes contentious, sometimes comforting compromise between honoring the dead and moving on."[49] Some critics decried the cookie-cutter doughboy statues and the traditional

---

49   Shanken, Andrew M. "Planning Memory: Living Memorials in the United States during World War II". *The Art Bulletin* Vol. 84, No.1 (Mar. 2002). pp. 130-147.

WAR MEMORIAL AND OPERA HOUSE, CIVIC CENTER, SAN FRANCISCO, CALIF.   24

Brown and Lansburgh, *San Francisco War Memorial and Opera House*, 1932. Postcard.

memorials as "tawdry monumental monstrosities." Other reactions were bound up in a generalized distaste for the past and the post-war urge to get back to normal. The need to re-plan cities to accommodate the auto also decreased the space available for traditional monuments. Still another criticism was that the sheer horror of the Holocaust and the atomic bombs overwhelmed the capacity of traditional monuments to commemorate.

Indeed, one month after the atomic bombs were dropped on Japan, the architect Philip Johnson scornfully proposed that the most suitable monument would be a massive mound of dirt. This action, he wrote, "offer[ed] a unique opportunity for that most American of modern tools, the bulldozer, which could build mounds many times the size of the pre-historic ones in considerably less time …"[50]

The urban critic Lewis Mumford, who had lost a son in World War II's Italian campaign, gamely defended traditional monuments. According to Mumford, the proper form of memorialization "cannot be achieved by an auditorium or a swimming pool, perfunctorily named a memorial. These useful structures do not bind us to the dead; they do not stir feelings and rouse the energies that will keep us from being content with such debilitated efforts as would merely give us the illusion of 'peace in our time.' That higher function and that higher purpose belong to the sphere of art, and such art

---

50   Johnson, Philip. "War Memorials: What Price Aesthetic Glory?" *Art News* (44) Sept. 1945, p. 25.

is essentially of a religious character."[51] But Mumford's voice was a lonely one.

As Shanken continues: "With World War II, American rituals of commemoration began to lapse into excuses for leisure activity with only nominal gestures, a plaque, or a sign, to memory."[52] In 1968, Congress voted to change Washington's Day, Memorial Day, and Veterans Day to the nearest Monday to permit more three-day weekends. One sponsor argued that such holidays would "improve the lot of all our citizens, smooth the paths of commerce, benefit the working man, save money for the country, and possibly lives, and it will not cost the government a penny."[53] Veteran outrage, however, forced the government to return Veterans Day to November 11.

Even without the dilution of commerce, living memorials seemed to carry the seeds of their own destruction, or at least relevance. The longer people used them for ordinary, non-memorial purposes, the less they remembered the original object of homage. But living memorials were not dead yet. They still had a place in the toolbox of public commemoration.

BLUE STAR MEMORIAL HIGHWAY
A tribute to the Armed Forces that have defended the United States of America

Blue Star Highway Sign, Interstate 81, Virginia.

True living memorials invite interaction, participation. They involve encounters, rituals, and pilgrimages. One walks through a grove, an arbor; one touches a stone. Living memorials turn the viewer into an active partner in commemoration. The mourner becomes a celebrant.

One modern example of just such a "true" living memorial is the phenomenon of Civil War re-enactors. The living replace the dead as the most important element on the battlefield. Instead of "little noting" what the real troops did on any given battlefield, the emphasis changes to what the play-soldiers do there. Figuratively, they pull down the marble soldiers from the pedestals and out of the bas reliefs, don their clothing with varying degrees of authenticity, eat, growl, spit, and snarl like the real McCoy. In every engagement, they experience Churchill's famous assertion that "There is nothing more exhilarating than to be shot at with no result." The re-enactors have at times gotten so carried away with their drama that they complained that the statues of real soldiers obstruct their fake battles!

A second monument that deserves the "living memorial" status is Maya Lin's Vietnam Veterans Memorial in Washington, DC. The closer you come to its black Bangalore marble, the more it resolves into a mixture of the names of the dead and a reflection of you, the visitor. The interaction of memorializer and memorialized is transfixing. In a brilliant

---

51   Mumford, Lewis. "Monuments and Memorials," *Good Housekeeping* 120 (Jan. 1945) p. 107.

52   Shanken, p. 141.

53   Meskill, Thomas J., Edward Boland, and Peter Rodino. *Congressional Record, U.S. Congress, House.* 90th Congress, 2nd sess. 9 May 1968, 114, pt. 10: 12583-12612

Vermont Civil War Hemlocks Re-enactors, *Battle of the Wilderness*. (Photo courtesy of Vermont Civil War Hemlocks)

stroke, Lin went one better than Lutyens' *Thiepval Monument to the Missing* by putting the names of the dead in chronological order, so that the visitor can find that father, son, brother, or cousin or friend in history.

Further, Lin invited the living to walk into the "tomb" to "touch" the dead and be healed. She wrote: "I don't make objects: I make places. I think this is very important—the place sets a stage for experience and for understanding experience."[54] The names rise off the surface like re-embodied spirits. Each name looses dikes of memory, which flow out to the living. In the film documentary about her, Lin spoke of the monument's cathartic intent: "We have to remember the people first, not the politics.... Only when you accept the pain can you overcome it. As you read a name or touch a name, the pain will come out."[55]

At least two legitimate uses of the term "living memorial" grew out of the terror attacks of September 11, 2001. The 9/11 Living Memorial Project of Voices of September 11 described itself as an online interactive tribute commemorating the lives and preserving the stories of September 11. Later on, the project expanded its mission to "include nonpartisan advocacy for public policy reform on prevention, preparedness, and response related to terrorism."

Secondly, at the urging of Congress, the US Forest Service created a "Living Memorial" project that invoked "the resonating power of trees to bring people together and creat[e] last living memorials to the victims of terrorism, their

---

54   From the film *Maya Lin: A Strong Clear Vision*, directed by Freida L. Mock, 1994.

55   Ibid.

Visitors, *Vietnam Veterans Memorial.*
Washington, DC.

families, communities and the nation."[56] In effect, they built upon the New York Botanical Garden's advocacy for trees and space after World War I. What's more, the Service created a national online registry of over 600 living memorials that could both document what had already been done and give ideas for what might be done in the future. Examples were open spaces, greenways, parks, schools, gardens, and forests. The Forest Service looked for projects that were "imbued with an ecological approach in process, design and maintenance" and considered these as "having higher potentials … for building trust and cooperation."

Just one of those examples was in Dracut, Massachusetts, home to Capt. John Ogonowski, the pilot of American Airlines Ft. 11, the first plane to crash into the World Trade Centers. In 2003, the Dracut Land Trust, a group Ogonowski helped found, bought thirty-three acres across from the family farm and made it an agricultural preserve forever. "One hundred, 200, 300 years from now, this land will still be producing crops," Ogonowski's brother Jim said at the dedication. .

The Civil War beckoned with another horticultural memorial project. The Journey Through Hallowed Ground Partnership committed to plant 620,000 trees from Charlottesville, Virginia, to Gettysburg, Pennsylvania; one for each of the estimated Civil War dead. The trees will be red sunset maples, chestnut and willow oaks, red-twigged dogwoods, red cedars and eastern redbuds. Advocates said, "We don't want another flagpole. We don't need another monument." Using GPS technology, the group is working with the National Park Service and other partners, including the online sites ancestry.com and fold3.com, to create an interactive map that will allow anyone traveling the route to find a tree planted for an individual soldier.

One of the best living memorials for almost 150 years has been at Harvard College. In the three years after the Civil War ended, the Harvard community raised a staggering $370,000—a sum equal to one-twelfth of the endowment of the University—to build Memorial Hall in honor of its war dead. President

---

56   "Living Memorials Project Summary." *USDA Forest Service.* Web. 28 Sep 2013. http://na.fs.fed.us/urban/living-memorials/LivingMemSummary.pdf

Above, *Conservation Area.* Dracut, Massachusetts. In memory of American Airlines pilot Captain John Ogonowski, killed on September 11, 2001.

Right, Ware and Van Brunt, *Memorial Hall and Sanders Theater*, 1870-77. Harvard University, Cambridge, Massachusetts.

Charles Eliot called the Hall "the most valuable gift the University has ever received, with respect alike to cost, daily usefulness, and significance." Architectural critic Douglass Shand-Tucci contends that, "as the preeminent architectural symbol in this country of the triumph of the anti-slavery crusade, its only rival is the Lincoln Memorial in Washington."[57]

The Memorial Transept between the Hall and Sanders Theater is sacred space, indeed. The marvelous stained glass windows high on the facing walls are the architectural cue that this is a religious edifice. The worn and uneven marble floor have the feel of an English cathedral or country church. On the wall are twenty-eight oak-framed marble plaques on which are carved the names of Harvard's 136 Civil War dead. They become a visual tolling of bells: CHARLES REDING-

---

57   Douglass Shand-Tucci. *Harvard University: The Campus Guide.* New York: Princeton Architectural Press, 2001. P.159

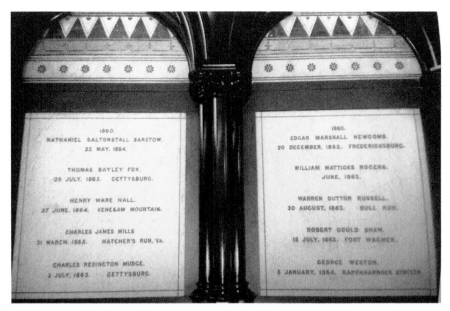

Ware and Van Brunt, *Memorial Hall Transept,* detail of marble tablets.

TON MUDGE, 3 JULY 1863 GETTYSBURG, EDGAR MARSHALL NEWCOMB, 20 DECEMBER 1862, FRED-ERICKSBURG, WARREN DUTTON RUSSELL, 30 AUGUST 1862 BULL RUN, ROBERT GOULD SHAW, 18 JULY, 1863, FT. WAGNER ....

Of this space, the novelist Henry James wrote, "a chamber, high, dim, and severe, consecrated to the sons of the university who fell....the effect of the place is singularly noble and solemn, and it is impossible to feel it without a lifting of the heart."[58]

A distinctive contemporary example of interaction between the public and a work of art stands on Platform One in London's Paddington Station is the Great Western Railway's War Memorial. *[See illustration, page 66]* For almost 100 years, a ten-foot tall bronze statue with an architectural surround depicts an unknown World War One soldier reading a letter. The Memorial by Charles S. Jagger honors the 2,524 employees of the Great Western Railway who died during the First World War. The memorial was unveiled on Armistice Day in 1922 by Viscount Winston Churchill. Jagger himself had been a member of the Artists' Rifles regiment, was wounded twice and awarded the Military Cross.

---

58   James, Henry. *The Bostonians.* New York: Modern Library, 2003.

As part of a nationwide cultural program of reflection about World War I, novelists Kate Pullinger and Neil Bartlett encouraged everyone in the UK to take a moment or two and imagine (and then write) the letter that the soldier was reading. Participants could then submit their letters to an interactive digital database. In the space of six weeks, the website received an astonishing 21,400 letters from people of all ages and walks of life. All of the letters collectively created a new living memorial of words. The letters will also be archived in the British Library.

In the fall of 2011, I went on a treasure hunt to Burlington's Memorial Auditorium, less than one mile from my house. I'd been in the building countless times for civilian activities. But what, I asked, were the *memorials* in Memorial Auditorium, and where were they?

In the spare, marble-floored foyer of the building I found eight large bronze plaques mounted on the walls with the names of hundreds of Burlington men who fought or died in World War I. A star next to a name indicated "The Supreme Sacrifice." Atop each plaque was the inscription: "Honor Roll of the city of Burlington World War One, 1917-1918." I scanned down the names, many of which are common still: BARROWS, BEAUPRE, BOIVERT, BOMBARD, BURNS... Cs, Ds, Es...to the Ms. There they ended. There were no Ns through Zs. Where were the rest? I looked around the second floor, the basement, the auditorium floor itself. Nothing. Had they been stolen? Custodians had no clue.

A month later, one custodian who had been on sick leave came forward to say that the plaques were in the basement under the stairs at the south end of the building—unceremoniously stacked like folding chairs and covered in dust. Each was heavier than a coffin, which had doubtless made them hard to steal. He thought they had been removed for some electrical work and never remounted.

I felt compelled to reach out to the Parks and Recreation Department, where the energetic new director was sympathetic but said the city had little money for restoration. I shared the story with a small group of World War II, Korean War, and Vietnam War-era veterans who were similarly interested in seeing the plaques re-hung. Several of us went to a local metal restoration company, who gave us an estimate of about $10,000. With help from The Preservation Trust of Vermont, our group of raised $8,000 in about three months. At this sign of diligence, the city chipped in the final $2,000.

As the crew from Conant Custom Metal worked on the plaques, we made three happy discoveries. In addition to the Burlington veterans named N-Z, we found a single plaque listing the Burlington women who had served in that war. There were also plaques with the names of Burlington's World War II, Korean War, and Vietnam War dead.

Thus, on Armistice Day, aka "Veterans Day" 2013, the Mayor and other dignitaries came and gave their blessings— ninety-five years after the Armistice was signed in Western Europe.

How joyful it was to see those last names back on the wall: YOUNGER, YUDAS, ZENO, ZURAWSKI—with a star next to Zeno's name for "The Supreme Sacrifice."

Missing World War I plaques as found in Burlington's *Memorial Auditorium* basement.

Conant Metal workers reburnish the bronze plaques.

Restored plaques are re-hung.

I was proud to work on this quirky triangulation of sinew and stone. I wasn't Hiram Bingham discovering Machu Picchu, but my journey was a satisfying bit of local participatory archaeology and history that breathed new life into a living memorial.

CHAPTER EIGHT

National Monuments of Commemoration: The United States, Great Britain, and Canada

"We set today a votive stone; that memory may their deed redeem"—Ralph Waldo Emerson, "Concord Hymn," 1836.

NATIONAL CAPITALS ARE centers of government where the political and judicial business of a nation is conducted. In those capitals, large open spaces invite the public to think grandly of the government. They are also the literal and symbolic centers of national identity where monuments and museums speak of the historical and cultural legacy of a country. Solemnity may reign momentarily, but these symbolic centers invite participation: they become spaces for parades, recreation, and commerce. In a broad sense, these national public spaces are living monuments—intertwining the honor of the past with the engagement of the present.

We will focus on those permanent monuments that have become gathering places for citizens and tourists. Their pilgrimages to the shrines of nationhood affirm their individual and collective political and cultural identities. In particular, we will look at three cities where the military monuments and memorials commemorate these anchors of sacrifice in grand public spaces. We examine the Mall and environs (including Arlington National Cemetery) in Washington, DC; Parliament Hill and environs on Wellington (including the nearby National War Memorial on Elgin) in Ottawa; and the area from Trafalgar Square down Whitehall to Westminster Abbey in London. Over time, these symbolic sites have become sacred in a secular way. There is no doctrine of *stare decisis* in public monument construction, spatially or emotionally. Through a jerky, accretive process of irregular wars, changing tastes, and often querulous political decision making, these monuments and memorials have come into being.

UNITED STATES

"America's capital with its extraordinary public landscape will always be the preferred setting for national monuments."
—Roger Lewis, 1996

Franklin Simmons, *The Peace Monument*, 1877-78. Civil War Sailors Monument, Washington, DC.

When French city planner Pierre Charles L'Enfant conceived and designed the Mall in 1791 as an uninterrupted park-like setting that would extend from the Capitol in the east to the Potomac River at the west end, the scale was far from pedestrian. Over time, the Mall has become a Champs-Élysees, with monuments to presidents and generals who defended the Union and to men and women of the armed forces who died in wars in defense of the country.

The Peace Monument

Designed by Franklin Simmons and originally intended for placement in Annapolis, Maryland, an allegorical work called the *Peace Monument* (1877) —also known as the Civil War Sailors' Monument—was the first monument to be completed in the vicinity of the Capitol. Placed near the *Grant Memorial,* the work takes it name from the allegorical depiction of Peace holding an olive branch. On the verso side, the figure of Victory extends a wreath. Above, the crowning figure of America weeps on the shoulders of History, on whose book is written, "they died that their country might live."

The Washington Monument

The first monument to be placed on the Mall was *The Washington Monument*. It is an Egyptian-inspired obelisk begun on July 4, 1848 to commemorate General and First President George Washington. The obelisk displaced an originally planned equestrian statue of Washington for the site. Situated roughly in the middle of the Mall, *The Washington Monument* is oriented towards the White House to the north and the Capitol building to the east. The construction of the monument was interrupted because of the Civil War and was not completed until December 6, 1884.

The Grant and Lincoln Memorials

In the United States, the unofficial national memorials to the American Civil War are the two national presidential monuments which cap the east and

Henry Schrady, *The Grant Memorial*, 1922.
Washington, DC.

west ends of the National Mall in Washington, D.C.. *The Grant Memorial* is placed in front of (and down the terraced hill from) the Capitol building facing the Capitol Reflecting Pool. *The Lincoln Memorial* faces the Capitol and the Reflecting Pool. Between the two is the first national presidential monument to General George Washington. The idea of juxtaposing Lincoln and Grant—who together "saved the Union"—was expressed earlier in their equestrian portraits placed on the inside of the *Soldiers and Sailors Arch* in Brooklyn in 1892. The interaction between the president and his general occurs as the result of their physical proximity. They engage each other. On the Mall, however, the scale, placement, and the material expressions of the *Grant* and *Lincoln* Memorials—one a three-part bronze sculpture tableau, the other an architectural temple with seated statue in marble—make such a direct connection between the two visually impossible. It is a symbolic interaction only.

The US Congress finally approved the funds and the site for the presidential memorial to Abraham Lincoln in February 1911, having earlier approved the incorporation of the Lincoln Monument Association in 1867. The delay in building a national memorial to Lincoln—a delay similar to that of Washington's monument—can be explained by the construction of other monuments to the president which took precedence.[59]

The design competition for *The Lincoln Memorial* in 1912 pitted distinguished architects John Russell Pope and Henry

---

59   *The Lincoln Tomb (1868-1874)* erected in Lincoln's hometown of Springfield, Illinois, was designed by sculptor Larkin Mead, whose elaborately terraced monument featured an obelisk rising 117 feet, against which is placed a statue of the president. Thirteen years later, Augustus Saint-Gaudens completed the *Abraham Lincoln Monument (1887)* for Lincoln Park in Chicago. A pensive, standing Lincoln grasps his lapel with his left hand, having just risen from his presidential chair. Lincoln's pose and expressive modeling contributed to the popular success and national recognition of the work by the crowds attending the Chicago Worlds Fair of 1893. Although the work remains one of the most popular sculptures of Lincoln, it is not the national monument erected by the government to the martyred president.

William O'Donovan and Thomas Eakins, *Equestrian Portrait of General Grant*, 1892. Soldiers and Sailors Monument, Grand Army Plaza, Brooklyn, New York.

William O'Donovan and Thomas Eakins, *Equestrian Portrait of Abraham Lincoln*, 1892. Soldiers and Sailors Monument, Grand Army Plaza, Brooklyn, New York.

Bacon against one another. The latter won the competition, and Bacon collaborated with sculptor Daniel Chester French. The idea was to create a massive seated Lincoln within a Greek Temple with Roman attic. Thirty-six doric columns representing the thirty-six states at the time of Lincoln's death would stand on the exterior. The design is most closely related to the Parthenon on the Athenian Acropolis with its cult statue of Athena Parthenos. French depicts the seated Lincoln in formal dress with a long flowing coat, his hands gripping the sides of his chair (throne). He is looking ahead with resolve and confidence—an image of a wise and determined president who has saved the Union. French's Lincoln—nineteen feet high and wide—is carved in white marble; it is the psychological Civil War parallel and counterpart to the sculptor's life-size Revolutionary War image of *The Minuteman* cast in bronze. Carved on the wall in back of the seated Lincoln are the words: IN THIS TEMPLE AS IN THE HEARTS OF THE PEOPLE FOR WHOM HE SAVED THE UNION THE MEMORY OF ABRAHAM LINCOLN IS ENSHRINED FOREVER. This message gives credence to the sculptor's dramatic rendering of Lincoln as Biblical patriarch, Greek god, and enshrined saint. Lincoln's Second Inaugural Address and his Gettysburg Address are carved on the north and south walls.

Daniel Chester French, *Abraham Lincoln,* 1922. The Lincoln Memorial, Washington, DC.

Henry Schrady, *Equestrian Portrait of Ulysses S. Grant*, 1922. The Grant Memorial, Washington, DC.

As an architectural monument, *The Lincoln Memorial* continues the Greco-Roman vocabulary expressed earlier in the White House and the US Capitol; a language that Thomas Jefferson originally embraced as the appropriate architectural expression of the newly formed democracy. Its placement orients the monument to the Lee Mansion in the Arlington National Cemetery to the south, and to the Washington Monument, the Grant Memorial and the US Capitol to the east. The Reflecting Pool almost a third of a mile in length mirrors the Memorial with its steep stairs and elevated podium from which major speeches, events, and celebrations of national significance have taken place. Almost a mile away on the Mall to the east, Lincoln's gaze falls on General Grant, who secured the peace and ended the Civil War.

Ulysses S. Grant, like George Washington, was both a military hero and a president (the sixteenth) of the United States. Congress approved the funds for a memorial to Grant in 1902. It was originally to be placed on the oval enclosing the White House. There were twenty-seven entries to the design competition; the winners were sculptor Henry Merwin Shrady and architect Edward Pearce Casey, the latter one of the architects of the Library of Congress. The success in 1901 of Shrady's imposing equestrian statue of *General George Washington at Valley Forge* for the Continental Army Plaza in

Henry Schrady. *Artillery Group*, 1922. The Grant Memorial, Washington, DC.

Henry Schrady, *Cavalry Group*, 1922. The Grant Memorial, Washington, DC.

Brooklyn most likely influenced the judges' decision to award the project to him.

The Grant Memorial consists of a tripartite bronze ensemble resting on a Vermont marble platform over 250 feet in length. General Grant sits erect on his horse Cincinnati; a full-length military cloak is draped around him as he looks calmly west toward the Lincoln Memorial. The scale is imposing: the equestrian statue rises over seventeen feet high and rests on a marble pedestal more than twenty feet high. The pedestal includes bronze relief insets of marching troops on either side, reminiscent of Saint-Gaudens' marching troops in his *Shaw Memorial* in Boston.

To Grant's left and right, groups of militia—Artillery and Cavalry Charge—are depicted on elevated marble pedestals. These life-size tableaus recall the expressive and active designs of Shrady's better known contemporary, the sculptor/illustrator Frederic Remington, in their depiction of horses, wagons, men, flags, and weapons in active combat. What some contend is a self-portrait of Shrady appears under the horses' hooves in the Cavalry sculpture. Shrady died before the memorial's dedication on April 27, 1922—the one hundredth anniversary of Grant's birth. Its final placement in front of the Capitol reflecting pool mirrors the Lincoln Memorial with its reflecting pool. The two Presidential memorials symbolically function as a national Civil War memorial.

The Amphitheatre and the Tomb of the Unknown Soldier

The gravestones of unknown American soldiers who died in the Great War and were buried in cemeteries overseas were marked with the inscription "Unknown." France and Great Britain simultaneously created national monuments to their unknown dead in their respective capitals; France beneath the Arc de Triomphe in Paris and Great Britain in Westminster Abbey, London. Both were dedicated on November 11, 1920. The United States dedicated its *Tomb of the Unknown Soldier* the following year, also on Armistice Day. The selection on October 24, 1921 at the Hôtel de Ville in Châlons-sur-Marne, France, from among four bodies of unknown America soldiers buried in the four military cemeteries in France was somber and ritualized. The body finally selected was placed aboard the American cruiser *Olympia* in Le Havre, and it arrived in Washington, DC, on November 9. It was placed on view in the Rotunda of the Capitol the next day. On November 11, 1921—three years after the end of the Great War—the casket was processed to the Memorial Amphitheatre in Arlington National Cemetery. After the completion of a formal ceremony overseen by President Warren Harding, the casket was placed in a simple sarcophagus of white marble on the east stairwell in front of the amphitheatre.

The Amphitheatre, with its Greco-Roman inspired apse and colonnade designed by Thomas Hastings and Frederick D. Owen, was begun in 1915 and completed in 1920. It was constructed of white marble from the Danby quarries in Vermont and replaced an earlier structure of wood. The original *Tomb of the Unknown Soldier* was also constructed of Danby marble. The later addition to the 1921 sarcophagus was designed by sculptor Thomas Hudson Jones together with architect Lorimer Rich. Doric pilasters stand at the corners, and the front panel faces the city of Washington. It depicts in low relief three Grecian figures representing Peace, Victory, and Valor. Victory wreaths adorn the other three sides, and the inscription facing the Memorial Amphitheatre reads HERE RESTS IN HONOURED GLORY AN AMERICAN SOLDIER KNOWN BUT TO GOD. The Honor Guard for the Tomb changes hourly throughout the year (on the half hour from April 1 to September 30). The disciplined ritual of the Changing of the Guard is reverently admired by millions of visitors each year.

Twentieth-century Monuments and Memorials on the Mall

In the twentieth-century, the Mall became a repository for monuments and memorials to service men and women who fought and fell in the many wars in which the United States was engaged. As James Reston, Jr. glibly noted in 1995, "Every war, it seems, now has to have its own triumphal memorial."[60] Given the limited size of the Mall and its "preferred setting for national monuments," architect and critic Roger Lewis noted, " one can visualize it being cluttered with memorials during the next century. What then would remain for the centuries to follow?" [61]

---

60   James Reston, Jr. "The Monument Glut." *The New York Times*. 10 Sep 1995.

61   *Lewis, Roger K.* "Washington Monuments: Battles over the Mall." *Architectural* Record 184, no. 1 (January *1996*): 17–21.

Rich and Jones, *Tomb of the Unknown Soldier*, 1915-20. Arlington National Cemetery, Alexandria, Virginia.

Brooke,Peaslee, and Wyeth, *National First World War Memorial,*1931. Washington, DC.

To look at the four existing war memorials on the Washington Mall is to see art, bureaucracy, and democracy in an uneasy alliance. Forming a trapezoid, the first of the quartet is the most self-effacing and traditional. Recalling Bramante's *Tempieto* (1502) in Rome and itself a probable influence on the later *Jefferson Memorial*, the *First World War Memorial* was authorized by Congress in 1924, completed in 1931, and dedicated by President Herbert Hoover on Armistice Day of that year. The memorial is a simple but elegant circular domed Doric Temple with twelve twenty-two foot fluted marble columns resting on a low podium. It was the first war memorial to be placed on the Mall, and it was initially erected to commemorate the 499 troops from the District of Columbia who died in the Great War. In the cornerstone is a list of the 26,000 Washingtonians who served in that war. In 2011, it was officially designated the National First World War Memorial.

Fifty yards away lies the bombastic and sprawling *National Monument to World War Two* (2001-2004). The inspiration is also Italianate but from the era of Mussolini rather than the Renaissance. The original design proposed a 70,000 square foot underground museum with huge berms, which would have obscured visitors' views of the Capitol and part of the Washington Monument. As completed, its neo-baroque design—with triumphal arches and an elliptical reflecting pool and fountain surrounded by fifty-six pillars—was viewed by one critic as "vainglorious … .full of trite imagery."[62]

---

62   Thomas M. Keane, Jr. *Boston Herald*, May 25, 2004

Above, Frank Gaylord, *Korean War Veterans Memorial*, 1992-95. Washington, DC

Right, Friedrich St. Florian, *National World War II Memorial*, 2001-2004. Washington, DC.

The *Korean War Veterans Memorial* (1995) forms the third point on the trapezoid. It too suffers from a lack of simple, coherent design. Instead, its many components include pathways, grassy groves, a reflecting pool, and a wall with shadowy faces incised on its surface. Its strongest elements are the nineteen ghost-like soldiers on patrol wearing full military uniforms and ponchos. These were sculpted by Vermont artist Frank Gaylord. Not placed on pedestals, these life-size figures are "down to earth" and disturbing as they occupy the same ground plane and space as the viewers who confront them.

The closing point of the trapezoid and the best of the four war memorials on the Mall is the *Vietnam Veterans Memorial* (1982) designed by Maya Lin while she was a graduate student at Yale University. The Memorial has lived through storms of controversy befitting the most divisive war in America's history. To many veterans, the deep black granite "wings" were an insult to their service. They couldn't see the tribute there, or the symbolism. In time, veterans came to appreciate its starkness and learned to live with its powerful ambiguity. Ultimately, the abstraction disappeared in the overwhelming simplicity of 58,195 names, but for many veterans that did not happen until a second memorial—more literal in execution—of three soldiers in battle uniform by Frederick Hart was commissioned in 1984 to accompany Lin's abstract wall.

Maya Lin, *Vietnam Veterans Memorial*, 1982. Washington, DC.

Frederick Hart, *The Three Soldiers*, 1984. Vietnam Veterans Memorial Fund, Washington, DC.

The controversy of the Vietnam Veterans Memorial underscores the observation of architect Roger Lewis that "choosing a memorial design is an arduous and contentious process because it involves a diverse citizenry with diverse points of view. How much easier during past centuries when only a single patron had to be courted and satisfied."[63]

GREAT BRITAIN

"The Cenotaph's design is modest in character, and today it is such a familiar part of Whitehall that few persons who pass by stop to contemplate its significance, the curious circumstances of its creation, or the subtlety of its architectural lines."
—Allan Greenburg, 1989

---

63   Personal communication to the authors.

Whitehall: The Cenotaph to Westminster Abbey

The parade route from Trafalgar Square to Westminster Abbey via Whitehall—with its commemorative memorials and monuments—functions culturally and symbolically like the Mall in Washington, DC. *Nelson's Column* in Trafalgar Square was raised in 1843 to commemorate Admiral Horatio Nelson who died at the Battle of Trafalgar in 1805 having defeated the French and Spanish Fleets during the Napoleonic Wars. The monument stands 169 feet high. The seventeen-foot high figure of Nelson is dressed in full naval regalia. *Nelson's Column* dominates the great public space designed in the early nineteenth century by architect John Nash. It is a gathering place for public events and festivals similar to the area in front of the Lincoln Memorial in Washington. Fountains, guardian lions, and three plinths with statues also honoring military heroes define the square. A fourth plinth has become the stage for contemporary "faux monuments" of considerable wit and imagination. Trafalgar square and its towering statue function first and foremost as commemorative memorials to both an individual (Nelson) and to the supremacy of the Royal British Navy in the early nineteenth century.

From Trafalgar Square to the Houses of Parliament, one travels along Whitehall, the area paralleling the Thames River and formerly defined by the Palace of Whitehall, most of which burned in the Great Fire of 1699. Historic buildings (Inigo Jones Banqueting Hall), horse guards, and government offices including the prime minister's residence at Downing Street line both sides. Monuments to individuals of military fame from the mid-nineteenth and twentieth centuries are placed along Whitehall. Ivor Roberts-Jones' impressive statue of Winston Churchill (1973) in Parliament Square anchors the route of commemoration starting with the Nelson monument.

The Cenotaph

The most celebrated of the commemorative monuments placed along the parade route (and placed in the middle of the street) is *The Cenotaph* designed by Sir Edwin Lutyens, the prolific architect employed by the Imperial War Graves Commission. First erected in July 1919 as a temporary structure of plaster and wood for the Peace Celebrations following the signing of the Peace Treaty at Versailles—as was the catafalque near the Arc de Triomphe in Paris—the permanent memorial was erected the following year to commemorate the fallen of the British Empire in the Great War buried abroad. The permanent version was completed in 1920. A stone coffin rests on top of dressed Portland stone. Carved laurel wreaths adorn the top and ends of the monument, each side displaying three cloth flags representing different branches of the military and the Union flag. On each end is inscribed words chosen by Rudyard Kipling, THE GLORIOUS DEAD. The monument was well received. Prime Minister Lloyd George wrote to Lutyens within a week of the unveiling thanking him for "designing and building the memorial which has become a national shrine, not only for the British Isles, but also for the whole Empire."[64]

---

64 Christopher Hussey, "The Life of Sir Edwin Lutyens," London: Country Life, 1953. p.394

Railton, Baily, and Landseer, *Trafalger Square with Nelson's Column*, 1840-43. London. (Photograph courtesy of Wikimedia Commons)

Sir Edwin Lutyens, *The Cenotaph*, 1920. London.

Lutyens' design utilizes the principal of entasis to create a dynamic optical effect of slightly curving surfaces; the same principle was used by Lutyens in his design for the altar-like *Great Stone* for the IWGC cemeteries. Remembrance Day celebrations—the Sunday closest to November 11—are annually held at *The Cenotaph,* as are other military celebrations throughout the year. As art historian Allan Greenberg noted, "In some mysterious way the design of the Cenotaph embodied the nation's deep and terrible bereavement. It became the focus for the outpouring of four years of pent-up sorrow which had been waiting for victory, or some tangible signal, to be released."[65]

Critic C. Lewis Hind, writing in the December 16, 1925 issue of *The Outlook* went further. "The Cenotaph in Whitehall," he wrote, "is idealism-spiritual. The Royal Artillery Memorial, at Hyde Park Corner, by [Charles]Jagger, another work of genius, is realism-material. A howitzer in stone dominates the bronze figures. It is a warning against war. Art can

---

65   Allan Greenberg, "Lutyens' s Cenotaph," JSAH Vol.48.N.1[March,1989]

be a warning as well as a remembrance. We raise our hats when we pass the Cenotaph. We clinch our fists before the howitzer. We close our eyes and lift our hearts during the Two Minutes' Silence [On Remembrance Day]." It is, however, The Cenotaph, not the Royal Artillery Memorial, which is seen as Great Britain's National War Memorial to the Great War. Its design has been replicated with variations in cities throughout the former British Empire from Canada to New Zealand.

Tomb of the Unknown Warrior in Westminster Abbey

The *Tomb of the Unknown Warrior in Westminster Abbey* was dedicated the same day as *The Cenotaph*. King George V led the distinguished procession as it made its way to Westminster Abbey down Whitehall, slowly marching to Handel's "Funeral March" from *Saul*.[66]

Buried at the west end of the nave, the tomb is covered with a slab of black marble from Belgium, which bears the inscription, BENEATH THIS STONE RESTS THE BODY OF A BRITISH WARRIOR UNKNOWN BY NAME OR RANK BROUGHT FROM FRANCE TO LIE AMONG THE MOST ILLUSTRIOUS OF THE LAND AND BURIED HERE ON ARMISTICE DAY 11 NOV. 1920. IN THE PRESENCE OF HIS MAJESTY KING GEORGE V HIS MINISTERS OF STATE THE CHIEFS OF HIS FORCES AND A VAST CONCOURSE OF THE NATION THUS ARE COMMEMORATED THE MANY MULTITUDES WHO DURING THE GREAT WAR OF 1914-1918 GAVE THE MOST THAT MAN CAN GIVE LIFE ITSELF FOR GOD FOR KING AND COUNTRY FOR LOVED ONES HOME AND EMPIRE FOR THE SACRED CAUSE OF JUSTICE AND THE FREEDOM OF THE WORLD THEY BURIED HIM AMONG THE KINGS BECAUSE HE HAD DONE GOOD TOWARD GOD AND TOWARD HIS HOUSE.

Biblical inscriptions from both the Old and New Testaments of the Bible are inscribed around the main text. The entire monument is encircled with red poppies, the emblem of Remembrance Day in Commonwealth countries. Poppies symbolizes the blood shed on the fields of Flanders in the Great War; a reference to John McCrae's poem, "In Flanders Fields." The significance of the Tomb's placement—just inside the main entrance to the Abbey, where one is immediately confronted with the memorial—is obvious.[67]

---

66   The elaborate ceremony and ritual used in choosing the unidentified British soldier to be brought back to London for burial, and the pomp and military protocol employed established the precedent the United States used for the burial of its Unknown Soldier.

67   Sadly, a considerable admission charge must now be paid for admission—with the exception of residents of the Borough of Westminster.

CANADA

"The Government feels that a monument should be erected in the Capital of Canada ... to the memory of those who participated in the Great War and lost their lives in the service of humanity. It is the spirit of heroism, the spirit of self-sacrifice, the spirit of all that is noble and great that was exemplified in the lives of those sacrificed in the Great War ... it is that vision which the Government wishes to keep alive in erecting a monument of this kind." [68]

The National Commemorative War Memorial: "The Great Response"

Parliament voted to erect a National War Memorial in the 1923 session. "It is understood," Prime Minister King noted earlier in December, 1922, "that the monument should be symbolical in character and should be placed in the most central and commanding position in the capital. It has been suggested that in design and location something of the character of the famous Nelson monument in Trafalgar Square, London, would be appropriate." King proposed Connaught Place as the most appropriate site for the memorial, rather than Parliament Hill as some members of parliament had argued, because "there is already on Parliament Hill an impressive War Memorial in the Peace Tower." King was instrumental in changing the earlier name of the memorial from National Monument Commemorative of the War to National Commemorative War Monument. He argued, "The monument is really commemorative of the Canadians who participated in the war, not of the war itself."

A design competition notice for the memorial was sent out and by late June 1925, 120 designs were submitted. The entrants represented eight countries. Within several weeks, the field had been narrowed to seven, and by early January 1926, the successful winner of Canada's National Commemorative War Memorial was announced. The winner was English sculptor Vernon March, who already had several important public commissions to his credit. March died before the memorial was completed; his siblings finished the work over an eight-year period (1926-1932). First exhibited in 1932 in Hyde Park, London, to much public acclaim, it was shipped and reassembled with its granite pedestal and arch fabricated in Canada before its final unveiling by King George VI in Ottawa on May

18,1939. It is prominently situated at the intersections of Elgin and Wellington Streets. This is a public space bounded by the hotel Château Laurier, the post office, and the central railway station, with the Houses of Parliament to the west. Placed in the middle of Connaught Place—around which traffic (pedestrian and vehicular) moves—the placement of *The Great Response* is sited in a prominent urban space similar to *The Cenotaph* in London and the *Arc de Triomphe* in Paris.

Twenty-three bronze figures representing different branches of the Canadian military move through a granite arch atop of which are two bronze allegorical figures representing Peace and Freedom. These slightly larger draped figures,

---

68   Conditions of Open Competition, February ,1925, Department of Public Works, Ottawa. Canada.

Above, Vernon March, *The Response*, Detail, 1924-39. The National War Memorial, Ottawa.

Left, Vernon March, *The Response*, 1924-39. The National War Memorial, Ottawa.

according to March, "express the idea that they are alighting on the world with the blessing of Victory, Peace, and Liberty in the footsteps of the people's heroism and self-sacrifice who are passing through the archway below."[69] The military ensemble trudges behind a field gun drawn by two horses. The highly expressionistic treatment of the bronze figures and their forward movement over a rise sharply etched in silhouette as the viewer looks up to the work contrasts with the stark geometry of the grey granite arch. The total height of the monument is over seventy feet.

The Houses of Parliament and the Memorial Chamber (1916-1928)

"Tourists are flocking through the new Parliament buildings this summer. Some are from European countries, many hundreds from the United States and thousands from points in Canada. Most of the visitors leave ... deeply impressed."
—The Ottawa Journal, July 27, 1925

---

69   Quoted in The National War Memorial, Veterans Affairs, Ottawa, Canada.1982.

The Centre Block of the Houses of Parliament were partially destroyed by fire in February, 1916. In spite of the enormous expenditures allocated to the war, there was no hesitation about rebuilding. Architects John Pearson of Toronto and Jean Omer Marchand of Montréal were awarded the contract. Together they contributed to the redesign of the Center Block, appropriately utilizing the Gothic Revival style, which related to the buildings that remained.

Pearson was especially keen on creating a structure that would also symbolically function as a memorial to Canadians fighting in the Great War. His goal was achieved when the main tower of the newly rebuilt structure was designated by the Prince of Wales at the cornerstone laying ceremony on December 1, 1919 as the Tower of Peace.[70] The Ottawa Citizen, September 27, 1923, wrote that Pearson "has translated into the stone of the Peace Tower the ideals of the deathless Canadian army."

Standing 280-feet high with a carillon in the belfry, the tower is "embellished with figures of warriors with reversed arms on the exterior." It was Pearson who claimed that The Memorial Chamber within the tower was to be "the most fitting memorial to the Canadian Soldiers whose bodies lie buried in the soil of France." He lined the Chamber with materials from France and Belgium that he personally selected from places where the Canadian armies fought. In the Chamber's center is an altar of marble carved from a single block from Great Britain on which rests the Book of Remembrance (earlier called the Doomsday Book) containing the names of more than sixty thousand Canadians who died. A page of the book is ritually turned each day at the same time. Three stained glass windows designed by the Toronto firm of Cowan and Hollister adorn the Gothic-revival Chamber, with the themes of Remembrance, Call to Arms, and Dawn of Peace. The majority of the architectural carving was undertaken by American sculptor Ira Lake. The relief carving for the entrance tympanum to the Chamber is the work of Canadian Frances Loring. An elaborate iconography of carvings, inscriptions, and military heraldry traces the military history of Canada, although principally focused on the Great War. Originally, Pearson proposed that a Tomb of an Unknown Canadian Soldier be placed within the Memorial Chamber, but his proposal was rejected. As Colonel A.F. Duguid, the director of the Historical Section of the National Defense Headquarters has noted, "The Memorial Chamber has become the national shrine of Canada."

"Reconciliation": The Memorial to Peace Keeping, Ottawa (1992)

Known as the Peace Keeping Memorial, "Reconciliation" commemorates the participation of Canadian soldiers in the United Nations Peace Keeping Army, a global police force founded in 1948. Canadian Prime Minister Lester Pearson committed Canadian forces to the Army in 1956, noting, "We need action not only to end fighting but to make the peace … My own government would be glad to recommend Canadian participation in such a United Nations force, a

---

70   Known today at the Tower of Victory and Peace.

Marchand and Pearson, *The Tower of Victory and Peace*, 1916-22. Houses of Parliament, Ottawa.

Harman, Henriquez, and Oberlander. Reconciliation, *The Peace Keeping Monument*,1992. Ottawa.

truly international peace and police force." [71] The literal nature of its imagery—three carefully rendered soldiers in uniform, one woman and two men, atop a wall over which flies the Canadian flag—significantly departs from the traditional allegorical renderings of Peace usually depicted as a feminine, winged figure similar to Victory. Sited in the middle of Confederation Drive between Moshe Safdie's crystal palace (the National Gallery of Canada) and the heavily fortressed American Embassy, the *Peace Keeping Monument* seems marooned in its present location. Its intention is to honor those who died while serving in the UN forces, but the monument's conception and execution falls short of the transformation of images and materials necessary to function symbolically as a commemorative monument. Its placement away from Parliament Hill and Connaught Place lessens the work's status as "national monument."

In the future, the United States, Canada, and Great Britain will continue to erect monuments and memorials marking important national and global events. Where they will be erected and what form they might take are questions whose answers are complicated, owing to the complex process of decision-making by committee and the availability of public and

71   Lester Pearson quote inscribed on the *Peace Keeping Monument*, Ottawa, Canada.

private funding for such projects. In the recent past, public art and post-modernist architecture have tended to displace the more conventional figurative sculpture and classical architectural forms of commemoration. The "sacred spaces" have slowly but inevitably become filled up over time. New sacred spaces, as well as the perimeters of the older sacred spaces, will be the logical sites for such monuments. When the monuments and memorials are erected, they will function as benchmarks of *their* time and as lenses through which future generations will look once again at the accumulated events of the past to reshape their responses to them.

CHAPTER NINE

Coming Home: Vermont's Monuments, Memorials, and Commemorative Images

"In fifty years or so everyone who served in the War would be dead; and at some point after that, everyone who had known anyone who had served would also be dead. What if memory grafting did not work?"—Julian Barnes, "Evermore"

"Now, as then and always, Vermonters bear their full burden with an unfaltering and grim determination."
—Governor Horace F. Graham

WE BEGAN OUR book with an exploration of monuments in one place—Burlington, Vermont. We then traveled far to Ottawa, London, the Somme and the Marne, to Gettysburg and Antietam to touch on larger themes of burials, living monuments, and national spaces. Now, we return to explore the memorial landscape of our own state. Vermont has a rich and diverse legacy of grafted memory. It boasts a slew of solid contributions to the architectural and sculptural memorials of the past, many of which were crafted from Vermont's own granite and marble quarries. In our exploration of the construction of commemoration, we saw three physical actions performed by survivors and succeeding generations: encounters, rituals, and pilgrimages. Each is integral to the task of grafting memory. Now we bring home our wide-ranging enquiry into that project to examine various ways in which Vermonters have succeeded in that effort.

BATTERY PARK, BURLINGTON

On a bucolic summer's day, Burlington's Battery Park is full of peaceful activities: volleyball games, children on swings, families picnicking, joggers running to and fro, amateur musicians using the bandstand for their fifteen minutes of fame. The park offers a panoramic view of Lake Champlain with the Adirondack Mountains to the west. The "battery" in Battery Park refers to a unit of war-making artillery. In 1812, this six acre plot was an American battery of guns and encampment used to defend the city and inlands against depredations by the British army sailing down the lake from Canada. The British shelled this promontory from gunboats a mile out in the lake. No artifacts from that war are evident, but two Civil War

Panoramic view of Battery Park with monuments and Lake Champlain. Burlington, Vermont.

Parrott naval siege guns point their defiant snouts out across the water ready for a Rebel attack.

At the southern end of the park stands a prominent Civil War figure. He is defiant but oftentimes defenseless—owing to the vandalizing of his sword. How many people stop to gaze at the statue of General William Wells, one of Vermont's heroes at Gettysburg, on which battlefield there stands an identical statue? Even among those who notice Wells' heroic pose, few will pause to peer at the bas relief of the Wells-led cavalry charge on the base of his statue.

Twenty meters away from the Wells monument is a fenced-in area about five feet square surrounding a stone dedicated to the memory of Howard William Plant. He was the first enlisted man from Burlington to be killed in World War I. He was seventeen. A brass plate reads:

> *Dedicated to the memory of*
> *Howard William Plant*
> *Born July 25, 1900*
> *Enlisted in the US Navy June 8, 1916*
> *Wireless Operator US Destroyer Jacob Jones*
> *Torpedoed at sea December 6, 1917*
> *First Burlington Boy to die in the World War*

J. Otto Schweitzer, *Cavalry Charge*, 1914.
Detail from William Wells Monument,
Battery Park, Burlington, Vermont.

In between the Wells and Plant monuments is a surplus World War II 75 mm pack howitzer. It stands about the size of a riding lawn mower. On its base is an inscription which reads: Presented by Veterans of the 172nd Regiment of the 43rd Infantry Division in Memory of Their Fallen Comrades of World War II.

Battery Park can thus be viewed as a microcosm of one of the recurring themes of the book. The collective monuments of the park can be viewed as the accretions of history, placing both a burden and obligation upon the citizen as well as reminding them how subsequent history can often efface the past. It is probably inevitable, as historian Michael Kammen writes, that "societies reconstruct their pasts rather than faithfully record them, and they do so with the needs of the contemporary culture clearly in mind---manipulating the past in order to mold the present."72 It is, however, the encounter and ritual of Veterans Day celebrations in the park that help to graft the memories from one generation to the next.

Rituals and encounters of individuals and families with veterans who have been buried in local cemeteries are also acknowledged, both with the placement of flags by the gravestones on Veterans Day or flowers on Memorial Day in the spring.

---

72   Michael Kammen, *Mystic Cords of Memory*, New York: A.A. Knopf, Inc. 1991, p. 3.

139

Veterans Day Celebration, *Platt Monument*, n.d. Battery Park, Burlington, Vermont.

Monument to Howard William Plant, n.d. Battery Park, Burlington, Vermont.

CEMETERIES

> *Soldier, adieu; thy work is done;*
> *Sharp the contest, fierce the strife;*
> *The battle's fought, the victory won.*[73]

In one of the smallest state capitol cities—Vermont's Montpelier—lies one of the smallest national cemeteries in the country. The "Soldiers Lot" of 450 square feet contains eight gravestones. Those are some of the dead from the Sloan General Hospital established during the Civil War; a small number because many of the other patients either recovered or were taken home to their own towns for burial.

In almost every Vermont town cemetery are graves of Civil War veterans. Of the 35,000 Vermonters who enlisted in the Civil War, over 6,000 or 17 percent died. Only a few of the estimated war dead were retrieved by their families and

---

73 Tombstone inscription in Warren Cemetery; Warren, Vermont (courtesy of Deanna French).

Civil War Soldiers Lot (National Cemetery). Green Mount Cemetery, Montpelier, Vermont.

Highland Cemetery, Chelsea, Vermont.

brought home for burial. Most of the others were buried in national cemeteries in the rest of the country. The returning veterans who finished their natural lives in Vermont were buried in these local cemeteries. In Chelsea, one of the most beautiful cemeteries in Vermont crowns the town. Flags and Grand Army of the Republic medallions pepper the hill like spring daffodils. Among these lies the body of Captain Orville Bixby, whose stone lists the seventeen engagements he served in from Bull Run through Antietam, Savage Station, Fredericksburg, Gettysburg and on. He died in the furnace of the Wilderness. Nearby is the cenotaph of Daniel Skinner, who died at Andersonville. On the adjoining grave of his wife of fifty years are the words "God has marked every sorrowing day/And numbered every secret tear."

A strikingly different cry goes forth on a monument eighty miles north in the Greenwood Cemetery in St. Albans. To honor, lament, and condemn the death at Andersonville of his son, Joseph Brainerd erected a monument whose inscription in part reads that his son was "wholly neglected by President Lincoln and murdered with impunity by the Rebels, with thousands of our loyal soldiers by starvation privation, exposure and abuse."

At the back of the same cemetery are the graves of three of the more than eighty African Americans from Vermont who served in the Fifty-fourth Massachusetts Regiment; thirty-six enlisted men from that Regiment are known to be buried in Vermont. The Regiment was a distinguished group commemorated by Augustus Saint-Gaudens' *Robert Gould*

141

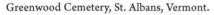

Greenwood Cemetery, St. Albans, Vermont.

Gravestone of Major General Oliver Otis Howard, Lakeview Cemetery, Burlington, Vermont.

Shaw Memorial on the Boston Common. Might the face of these Vermont soldiers be found in that memorial? Peter Brace, Alex Garrison, and Daniel Prince survived the war and are remembered in this cemetery with small, simple grave markers lined up in the same row.

In Lakeview Cemetery in Burlington, where we have already visited the grave of Gettysburg hero George Stannard, over 900 of the interred are Civil War veterans. One was Major General Oliver Otis Howard, who fought through the war, gained a Medal of Honor, and, like Stannard, lost an arm. At war's end, based upon his reputation as both hero and humanitarian, he was named the first commissioner of the Freeman's Bureau, a *de facto* social service agency established to help freed slaves obtain education, health care, and jobs. His grave is marked by no monument, no statue—only a cube of granite with his name and two stars.

LOCAL STATUES, HIDDEN IN PLAIN SIGHT

Like every other state, Vermont has its share of monuments hidden in plain sight, as we have noted in a previous chapter. Some of the towns borrowed the Antietam model (Old Simon), but a few like St. Johnsbury ("America" by Larkin Mead) and Swanton ("Goddess of Liberty" by Daniel Perry) chose to represent the sacrifices of the local citizens with feminine allegorical representations. Perry's carving is unusual in its proportions and distinctive in its use of local marble extracted from quarries in nearby Isle La Motte and Rutland.

As one drives along Grand Army of the Republic Memorial Highway Route 15 in Colchester, one sees a different standing sentinel—a life-sized granite statue of Captain (later Colonel) Donald Cook, US Marine Corps, who died in a North Vietnamese prison camp in 1967. Cook, a graduate of Saint Michael's College in Colchester, was posthumously award the Congressional Medal of Honor. Although his body was never recovered, he is recognized in the memorial section of Arlington National Cemetery. Nearby, but less visible owing to its placement at the Vermont National Guard Camp Johnson, is *The Fallen Warrior Memorial*—a monument placed nationwide that was erected at the beginning of the War on Terror.

VERMONT'S STATE HOUSE AS SACRED SPACE

There are many diverse elements that make this six-acre plot with its magnificent Statehouse Vermont's counterpart to the nation's capitol in Washington, DC. The Doric portico, the main ceremonial entrance, houses a granite statue of Vermont's ubiquitous Revolutionary hero Ethan Allen. One of the founders of the Green Mountain Boys, Allen was the commander of the troops that took Fort Ticonderoga without a shot and captured the cannon that became instrumental in the Battle of Boston. The current statue was carved in 1941 by Aristide Piccini to replace the original marble version carved by Larkin Goldsmith Mead in 1858. Next to Allen is a British cannon taken by American troops at the Battle of Bennington and probably used throughout the rest of the Revolution. Below the State House, like sailing outriggers, are two steel Krupp naval guns from the Spanish cruiser *Castilla,* which was sunk by Admiral George Dewey's squadron in Manila Bay, May 1, 1898 during the Spanish American war. As you stand in the foyer of the Statehouse, you behold a painting of Admiral Dewey—a Montpelier native best remembered for his phrase, uttered during the Battle of Manila Bay, "You may fire when ready, Gridley!" Directly down the hallway is displayed a portrait bust of President Abraham Lincoln, also sculpted by Larkin Mead. A third contribution by Mead is his carving of *Ceres* atop the Capitol's dome.

On the second floor, in front of the entrances to the House and Senate Chambers, one was previously able to see bunched Civil War battle flags. Now in storage, they are safely removed from harmful UV light. Thomas Waterman Wood's painting entitled *Return of the Flag* (1891) depicts many of those treasured flags. The painting now hangs in the Vermont History Center at the Vermont Historical Society in Barre.

Outside the Senate chamber is a bronze plaque to John Abner Mead, the fifty-third governor of Vermont. Mead was a physician, politician, businessman, and philanthropist who entered the war as a private in Company K of the Twelfth Vermont volunteers. With a sense of humility, his plaque boldly reads: "TO THE MEMORY OF THE COMMON SOLDIERS OF THE CIVIL WAR WHO WENT FROM VERMONT TO SAVE THEIR NATION"

The principal commemoration of the Civil War battle in which the most Vermont units were engaged is the painting by Vermont artist Julian Scott entitled *The Battle of Cedar Creek*. Commissioned by the legislature in 1870, the painting

Daniel Perry, *Goddess of Liberty*, 1868. Swanton, Vermont.

Statue to Donald Cook, Merrill Cemetery, Colchester, Vermont.

Fallen Warrior Memorial, Camp Johnson, Colchester, Vermont.

dominates a room known by the painting's title and which serves manifold functions. As John Singer Sargent's *Gassed* became one of the most iconic paintings from World War I, that role in Vermont's history was filled by "The Battle of Cedar Creek." It is an impressive twenty-by-ten-foot painting; Scott worked on it for four years. That engagement on Oct. 19, 1864 was the decisive battle of the Shenandoah campaign, and it was influential in the presidential election of 1864. Scott came from the northern Vermont town of Johnson and entered the Army at fifteen as a drummer boy, notably "under-

Ammi Young and Thomas Silloway, *Vermont State House*, 1833/1859. Montpelier, Vermont.

Larkin Mead, *Portrait Bust of Abraham Lincoln*, c.1870. Vermont State House, Montpelier, Vermont.

size and underage." He would win a Congressional Medal of Honor for rescuing soldiers at the Battle of Lee's Mills. After the war, Scott was classically trained in painting in New York City and Europe. His Cedar Creek masterpiece was deeply realistic. It was heroic but without bombast and included sympathetic renderings of Confederate prisoners.

PAINTINGS

Another more primitive pictorial rendering of that great battle is *Sheridan's Ride* at the Vermont Militia Museum on the Vermont National Guard base of Camp Johnson. This 17-foot by 28-foot painting on muslin was created in 1890 by Charles Hardin Andrus of Richford. It depicts the dramatic moment when General Philip Sheridan arrived after a twenty-mile ride to rally the dispirited troops and gain the day. Andrus was an itinerant scenic artist who

Bronze plaque to Governor John Abner Mead, Vermont State House, Montpelier, Vermont.

Julian Scott, *The Battle of Cedar Creek*, 1870. Vermont State House, Montpelier, Vermont.

painted theater curtains all over New England.

A more ambitious undertaking of that historic event by Andrus can be viewed at the Vermont Historical Society in Barre. Sections of the 150-foot long panorama of scenes that stretch from Fort Sumter through Kennesaw Mountain, Gettysburg and Cedar Creek to Appomattox are on display. Curiously, the final scene shows the Battle of Little Big Horn, where the impetuous Civil War hero George Custer and all his command were slain. Why Custer? Perhaps it was because Custer had led cavalry units at Cedar Creek and Andrus had already painted him prominently in the lower right quarter of the Militia Museum's *Sheridan's Ride*.

Other paintings and drawings of the Civil War whose purpose was to document and commemorate the common soldier can be found in the collections of the University of Vermont's Robert Hull Fleming Museum.[74] Julian Scott's me-

---

74　Photographs commemorating both individual soldiers, their companies, and regiments are included in the collections of the Vermont Historical Society in Barre (see the work of Vermont photographer George Houghton) and in the holdings of Special Collections at Bailey-Howe Library at the University of Vermont.

Charles Hardin Andrus, *Sheridan's Ride*, n.d. Collection, Vermont National GuardLibrary and Museum, Colchester,Vermont.

ticulous graphite drawing of a *Wounded Soldier* on the battlefield captures the moment with a faithful realism. This reflects Scott's successful academic training under Emmanel Leutze, whose best-known painting—*Washington Crossing the Delaware*, (1851)—documents an important event in the Revolutionary War. Also in the Fleming collection is Winslow Homer's moving preparatory drawing for the finished painting entitled *Trooper Meditating Beside a Grave* (1866), which is now in the Joslyn Art

Museum in Omaha. In a woodland setting, a lone soldier pauses and reflects on the death of a friend in arms, a pose reminiscent of both photographs and wood engravings from the era.

Thomas Waterman Wood, a Montpelier resident and a president of the National Academy, painted a moving triptych of an African American who joins the Union Army, is wounded, and returns home. Painted in 1866, the central panel—*The Recruit*—commemorates in paint the contributions of the individual soldiers who are collectively represented in The Robert Gould Shaw Memorial.

Thomas Waterman Wood, *A Bit of War History: The Recruit*, 1866, oil on canvas. Gift of Charles Steward Smith, 1884. Collection, The Metropolitan Museum of Art, New York City. (Image copyright The Metropolitan Museum of Art. Image source: Art Resource, NY)

Winslow Homer, *Trooper Meditating at a Grave*,1865, crayon and chalk on paper. Gift of Henry Schnakenberg. Collection, Fleming Museum of Art, University of Vermont, Burlington,Vermont.

Julian Scott, *Civil War Soldier*, c.1870, pencil and chalk on paper. Gift of George Benedict. Collection, Fleming Museum of Art, University of Vermont, Burlington, Vermont.

THE STONES OF VERMONT

From the fragility of canvas and paint, we turn to Vermont's two rocks of ages—marble and granite. The sources of many monuments and gravestones in Vermont's and the nation's war memory are the granite and marble quarries of Vermont in places like Graniteville, West Rutland, Proctor, and Dorset. "There is Barre granite somewhere on every Civil War battlefield in the country," says Vermont historian Howard Coffin. 75. As many as 300,000 marble gravestones for Civil War graves were quarried and carved in West Rutland. The speed of the process was greatly accelerated by the invention of the sandblasting machine, which became widely available in the early 1870s. Maya Lin's Vietnam Veteran's Memorial was fabricated and pieced together in 150 separate yet seamless panels at Natavi and Sons of Barre, Vermont. Monuments like the Tomb of the Unknown Soldier in Arlington National Cemetery and the World War I Memorial on the Mall in Washington, DC were made entirely of Vermont marble and to this day thousands of new gravestones for the national cemetery network are fabricated every year from Vermont stone.

Artisans and artists associated with the extractive industries of Vermont have also been tapped to contribute their talents in creating commemorative monuments and memorials both within and outside the state. Vermont is the home of Frank Gaylord, the sculptor of the Korean War Veterans Memorial, which is also on the Mall in Washington, DC. As a paratrooper in World War II, Gaylord fought at the Battle of the Bulge. After the war, he went to college on the G.I. Bill and fell in love with sculpture, noting that, "it was thrilling to carve something permanent."

The desire to work in granite brought Gaylord to Barre in 1951. There, he served apprenticeships with several companies as stonecutter, carver, sculptor, and designer. By 1957 he had set up his own studio, which freed him to do more interpretive work. When asked why he turned to public sculpture from gravestones, his answer was simple. "In a cemetery, your work was seen by perhaps six people twice a year," he said. But in a public space like the Washington Mall, his audience could be thousands in just a single day.

Vermont was one of the first states to sanction a memorial to Vietnam veterans. It was dedicated in 1992 and placed at the northbound rest area on Interstate 89 in Sharon.[76] That rest area could be considered a living memorial. To use the restrooms or to browse the rows of tourist brochures, you have to first walk through a kiosk that displays photographs of the Vermont soldiers killed in the wars in Iraq and Afghanistan. The Vermont Memorial to the Vietnam War commemorates the 120 Vermont soldiers who were killed in that conflict.

Vermont also created a Vermont Veterans Cemetery in 1992. By its very function and definition, this cemetery exemplifies the accretions of history, as does Battery Park in Burlington. And as is true of most cemeteries—rather than town greens or the honorific spaces of state and national Capitols—the ritual visitation by family and friends grasps

---

75   Nancy Price Graff, "In This State: A Little History of Those Ubiquitous Civil War Memorials," VTDigger, Feb. 24, 2013.

76   Interstate 89 is also designated the Vietnam Veterans Memorial Highway.

Francis Colburn, *Granite Quarry*, 1942, oil on canvas. Gift of the artist. Collection, Fleming Museum of Art, University of Vermont, Burlington, Vermont.

memory more securely.

The driving forces behind most commemorative monuments, memorials, and markers are the energy and dedication of one or two individuals. Let Retired Lieutenant Colonel Robert Walsh, USMC of South Burlington, Vermont, tell the story:

In my first term in the Vermont legislature, I was approached by a World War II veteran—Mr. Wayland Bowen of Richmond, Vermont—and asked if I would sponsor a bill to establish a Vermont Veterans Memorial Cemetery. I was surprised that Vermont didn't have one and thought it should have been done years ago. I agreed and had the legislative council prepare a draft, and then embarked on getting as many co-sponsors from both parties as possible. I think the final count was about twenty. The bill was introduced, sent to committee, and eventually passed by both the House and Senate. At that time, there were a number of veterans in the House and Senate who

Tim Smith and Associates, *Vermont Vietnam Veterans Memorial,* c. 2001. Interstate 89 rest area, Sharon, Vermont.

actively supported the bill—Representative Bob Wood of Brandon and Representative Bud Keefe of Rutland were particularly helpful. Representative John Zampieri supported the bill and later played a critical role in completing the project as commissioner of Buildings and Grounds.

We agreed the cemetery should be a final resting place that honored all veterans equally without regard for rank, achievements, or status. This continues to be the basic philosophy of the cemetery. Shortly after the cemetery was dedicated in 1993, Wayland approached me with the idea of raising funds for a chapel. I agreed on the condition that the chapel be nondenominational and serve as a place for quiet reflection and funerals. I then established a nonprofit organization with a Board of Directors. By 2004 we had raised sufficient funds and in-kind donations to build the chapel, and later the governor appointed me to the Veterans Cemetery Advisory Board. At this point we faced the first test of our philosophy. An effort was made to name the Chapel for a specific individual. The Ad-

Vermont Veterans Cemetery, Randolph, Vermont.

visory Board was successful in thwarting this effort and legislation passed that named the chapel "The Vermont Veterans Memorial Cemetery Chapel." I have continued to serve on the Advisory Board. I believe it is important for veterans to have a beautiful and dignified final resting place.

Acknowledgements

We wish to thank the following institutions:

American Battle Monuments Commission; Commonwealth War Graves Commission; Prints and Photographs Division of the Library of Congress, Washington, DC; the Metropolitan Museum, New York; the Tate Gallery, London; the Imperial War Museum, London; the National Gallery of Canada, Ottawa; the Canadian War Museum, Ottawa; the McCord Museum, Montréal; Library and National Archives of Canada, Ottawa; United States Archives, the Fleming Museum of Art, University of Vermont; Special Collections, Bailey-Howe Library, University of Vermont; the Vermont Historical Society; the Canadian Embassy, Washington, DC; and the University of Vermont for faculty research grants and sabbatical leaves.

And the following individuals for their help:

Raven Amori, Richard Bailey, Alan Bowness, Jesse Bridges, Kent Brown, Paul Carnahan, Faye Cheung, Howard Coffin, Emily Copeland, Prudence Doherty, Peter Fischer, Jim Fouts, Peter Francis, Frank Gaylord, Peter Gilbert, Chris Hadsel, Sara Leach, Tom Ledoux, Roger Lewis, Brad Limoge, Eric F. Long, Bill Metcalfe, Jane Naisbitt, Tim Nosal, Susan Ross, Chris Suthern, Julie Summers, William Spooner, Margaret Tamulonis, Kevin Thornton, Emily Wadhams, Bob Walsh, Lucinda Walker, and Ali White.

Unless otherwise credited, all photographs are by the authors.

About the Authors

Bill Lipke

A transplanted mid–westerner, Bill Lipke is professor emeritus of art history from the University of Vermont. He is a former director of the University's Fleming Museum of Art and a recipient of an Award of Merit from the Vermont Council on the Arts "in recognition of distinguished service to the arts in Vermont." Prior to his appointment at UVM, he held teaching positions at Cornell University and Reed College. His scholarly interests and publications range from the history of landscape painting to contemporary art and architecture. A proud father and grandfather, he resides in Burlington, Vermont. He is an avid sailor, singer, enthusiastic but amateur watercolorist, and long-time hospice volunteer.

Bill Mares

Raised in Texas, educated at Harvard, Bill Mares has been a journalist, high school teacher, and member of the Vermont House of Representatives. He has authored or co-authored 15 books on subjects ranging from the Marine Corps to workplace democracy to desert travel to Presidential fishing. His hobbies include running, beekeeping, singing, and fly-fishing. He lives in Burlington, Vermont with his wife of 44 years, Chris Hadsel. They have two sons.

CPSIA information can be obtained at www.ICGtesting.com
Printed in the USA
BVOW07s2014151015

422757BV00005B/6/P